Celebrate
the
SOLSTICE

Celebrate the SOLSTICE

Honoring The Earth's
Seasonal Rhythms
Through Festival and Ceremony

Richard Heinberg

Foreword by Dolores LaChapelle

QUEST BOOKS

The Theosophical Publishing House

Wheaton, IL U.S.A/Madras, India/London, England

The Theosophical Publishing House
P.O. Box 270
Wheaton, IL 60189-0270

A publication of the Theosophical Publishing House,
a department of the Theosophical Society in America.

*This publication made possible with
the assistance of the Kern Foundation*

Library of Congress Cataloging-in-Publication Data

Heinberg, Richard.
  Celebrate the solstice: honoring the earth's seasonal rhythms
through festival and ceremony/Richard Heinberg.
      p.   cm.
  Includes bibliographical references and index.
  ISBN 0-8356-0693-7 : $12.00
  1. Winter Solstice 2. Summer Solstice 3. Seasons — Folklore.
I. Title.
GT4995.W55H45   1993
394.2′6 — dc20   93-22750
                                                        CIP

9 8 7 6 5 4 3 2 1 * 93 94 95 96 97 98 99

This edition is printed on acid-free paper that meets the
American National Standards Institute Z39.48 Standard

Printed in the United States of America by Versa Press

The Solstice Wreath

The grim news has come to my attention
that something in the world has come unfixed—
owls no longer haunt the fir-lined alley
appearing out of dreamtime as we pass,

indeed, whole souls are missing, as if being
has itself gone dim—like an old man's seeing.
A vital light is missing from this world, by which I mean
that ephemeral gold that spins the seen

and unseen worlds together. In my life
I don't expect to see a springtime swelling
of the shriveled nut so many human spirits
have become. What's to be done?

This is the winter solstice of an age,
although the season's worst is yet to come.
What's delicate and true has come undone:
is the only fitting answer
a pure and focused rage?

Today I wove a wreath of bone and fir
and filbert withes; twined in sacred holly,
incense cedar from an ancient tree.
I wove, affixed a star, and spoke a spell:

"Let this circle stand as the gate of winter
sure passage to the days of lengthening light."
And then I whispered names in the fragrant bough
Lacing love like a scarlet ribbon through the fronds.

Long I wove and dreamed back friends and kin,
each great soul calling back the sun.
I thought at last, "My life here is not done."
and some bright star rekindled from within . . .

—Sandra Michaelson Brown

It is difficult to be religious, impossible to be merry, at every moment of life, and festivals are as sunlit peaks, testifying, above dark valleys, to the eternal radiance.

—Clement A. Miles

Rites, . . . together with the mythologies that support them, constitute the second womb, the matrix of the postnatal gestation of the placental *Homo sapiens*.

—Joseph Campbell

To celebrate a festival means: to live out, for some special occasion and in an uncommon manner, the universal assent to the world as a whole.

—Josef Pieper

By returning to the earth itself for the basis of our festivals, we include all the manifestations of Being wherever we live.

—Dolores LaChapelle

CONTENTS

Acknowledgments

Illustrations on page 116 are by Janet
Barocco; all others are by the author.

Cover artwork by Donnabeth Mitchell
Cover design by Beth Hansen
Book design by Richard Heinberg

The author wishes to thank Sandra Michaelson Brown for
permission to publish her poem, "The Solstice Wreath."

FOREWORD

SUMMER SOLSTICE marks the "turn-ing point" in the sun's yearly journey along our horizon. Just when the sun stays longest in the sky, it turns and begins its journey toward winter. For the ancient Chinese, Summer Solstice was the time when the earthly *yin* (female) energy is born and begins to wax strong while the sun *yang* (male) energy begins to wane in power. The balance was considered so delicate that everyone took great care to avoid any action which might upset this crucial turning point. No one traveled out of their own valley on the Summer Solstice.

Modern "scientific" thinking says we can't influence the sun. The sun, however, is not merely an object up in the sky; instead, the changing relationship between the sun and the Earth is the foundation of all life on Earth, and we are upsetting this precarious relationship.

"The sun is becoming darker," the Hopi, Loloma told us. "Every day there is less light." A few years ago he was invited to a Prince-ton University Convocation of Indian Scholars where everyone got up and made speeches about the problems of Indians and the future of America, but he thought they were ignoring the true problem. "I stood up and all I had to say were seven words," Loloma remembered with a smile. "In the East, there is no sun!" and he sat down. First there was silence; then everyone applauded. Ever-increasing pollutants in the air cut off some of the sunlight needed to grow plants and may eventually decrease the temperature enough to cause another ice age.

Meanwhile at the other end of the spectrum, we have problems caused by ultraviolet rays from the sun, unfiltered by the ozone layer in the stratosphere, which normally protects the Earth. Chlorofluorocarbons from air conditioners, fire extinguishers and other industrial sources are destroying this ozone layer. More ultraviolet light is already leading to increased skin cancer, cataracts and plant disease. We don't know what further damage may occur, because this invisible, protective ozone layer is what allows life to flourish on the Earth.

Through the years, our Western European industrial culture has belittled the superstitious "natives" who celebrate solstices and equinoxes to balance their relationship with the sun so that life could continue. But now we know not only how delicate this balance is but that humans do have a role in the relationship between the Earth and the sun.

Now that we are beginning to understand the damage we can do by continuing to ignore the human influence on the earth/sun balance, we need to find a way to begin to restore a healthy relationship with these greater powers. Since the earliest human cultures on earth, this way has been the celebration of the equinoxes and solstices. By celebrating together at these times, we balance the human community as well. A harmonious human community doesn't need consumer products to fill the empty hole in the psyche caused by a lack of real community. In *Celebrate the Solstice* we find out how many different cultures throughout the world have celebrated this day.

In dancing, we turn ourselves over to nature within, so that the narrow human ego with its insatiable needs is no longer in control. Richard Heinberg tells of the importance of dancing in the Solstice celebrations, and I want to add my experience to his.

On one Solstice our group made the decision to dance all night to the drums, finishing at dawn, not at sunrise, because looking directly at the sun may lead to blindness. When dawn came, however, small pink clouds began slowly moving over the top of the mountain. Everyone spontaneously turned to face that direction while continuing to dance in place. Not one person stopped, and the drumming, rattles and dancing increased. Just as the sun's upper rim cleared the mountain, everyone stopped moving, and all sound stopped instantly. There was not *one* extra beat. The entire group had been ritually synchronized to the point where it was enabled to act as a flock of birds turning together.

The resulting emotion was exuberant joy and overwhelming thankfulness that we had been "given" this opportunity of acting together with the rising sun and clouds and mountain. Thus we had our "share in the superhuman abundance of life . . . the fruit of the festival, for which alone it is really celebrated," in the words of the Austrian expert on ritual, Josef Pieper. He continues, "When a festival goes as it should, we receive something that it is not in the human power to give . . . the gift that is meant to be the fruit of the festival: renewal, transformation, rebirth."

Richard Heinberg asks, "Could there be a connection between our ignorance of the seasonal festivals, and our loss of relatedness with one another and with the Earth?" It is essential that we begin to comprehend, as Indians do, the psychological ecology underlying physical ecology. *Celebrate the Solstice* provides the necessary introduction.

Heinberg shows the importance of celebrating the Solstice where you live instead of "buying a plane ticket to London and then hopping a bus to Stonehenge." Moreover, he inspires us to spend the Solstice in our own place "consuming as little as possible of gasoline, electricity, and packaging." Most important of all, as Heinberg shows us, during the festivity of celebrating the Summer Solstice, we have the experience, unique in our culture, of neither *opposing* nature nor of *trying* to be in communion with nature but of *finding* ourselves within nature.

Because nature within us is part of the same great pattern as nature without, to begin the turn-around from "ravaged" land to "reverenced" land, the first step is to take time out to permit our inner patterns to re-align with the greater beings—the sun and the atmosphere—which give us our life here on Earth. *Celebrate the Solstice* shows us how to begin.

Dolores LaChapelle
Way of the Mountain Center

PART ONE

Earth Rhythms

Oh, what a catastrophe, what a maiming of love when it was made a personal, merely personal feeling, taken away from the rising and setting of the sun, and cut off from the magic connection of the solstice and equinox! This is what is the matter with us, we are bleeding at the roots, because we are cut off from the earth and sun and stars, and love is a grinning mockery, because, poor blossom, we plucked it from its stem on the tree of Life, and expected it to keep on blooming in our civilized vase on the table.

—D. H. Lawrence

CHAPTER 1

The Power of Festivals

IT IS AN EARLY WINTER MORNING in the year we would call 976, in the northeast corner of what is now San Fernando Valley in southern California. A Chumash shaman prepares for the most important moment of the season. He has spent the past three days fasting, singing, and praying. During the night he has partaken of the sacred and dangerous *datura* herb and his head reels with terrifying visions. Once again, as he has done every year at this time since receiving initiation from an older shaman, he deliberately crosses from the mundane world into the magical realm of the gods and spirits. He knows that this night, this morning, he must position himself at the boundary between the ordinary and the supernatural worlds in order to play his part in maintaining the balance and health of the Earth, of the sky, and of his people.

As the eastern horizon shows the first faint hint of coming daylight, he enters a shallow cave. Inside, he contemplates sacred petroglyphs whose meanings only he and his teacher understand. Dawn arrives, and the shaman watches in religious awe as a finger of sunlight approaches and bisects a series of concentric circles on the cave's back wall. It is only on one morning of the year—the morning of the year's shortest day—that this piercing of the circles occurs. It is a sign that the Sun has reached its extreme limit; it is a boundary of the cosmic order, revealing the shape of the world and of human affairs. Now, if his prayers have been effective, the days will grow longer and the light will return.

Later in the day he will lead his people in ceremony and celebration. The new year has begun, the Sun has been reborn, and the world has been fertilized.

▼ ▼ ▼

It is a summer night in seventeenth-century Cornwall. In every direction the horizon is lit up by hilltop bonfires. A young newlywed couple are dancing with their families and friends around a fire they've built from straw and brush. There is much laughter and singing. Each couple, hand in hand, takes a turn leaping across the flames for good luck, as Cornish couples have done on similar Midsummer evenings for untold generations past.

The young man and woman are from families with ancient ties to the land. In their entire lives they will never once leave this rugged precinct of tiny fields bordered by piled-rock fences, and dotted with prehistoric stone monuments—the subjects of innumerable and sometimes lurid legends.

This has been the longest day of the year. From this night onward until late December, nature will gradually lose her vitality, only to awaken again next spring with the return of the light.

According to the traditional English calendar, summer commenced on May 1; today, June 21, is Midsummer. Vegetation is nearly at its peak of growth; the wilting heat of late summer is yet to come. It is a time when local holy wells have special powers of healing, and when the ancient stone circles are visited by fairies and spirits.

The Church of England has repeatedly instructed the local priest to discourage Midsummer rites because of their "pagan" origin, but instead he turns a blind eye to them. Though he disapproves of all the talk of ghosts and nature spirits, he sees no

4

real harm in the festivities. After all, he can see for himself how the people are refreshed and revived by the break in their routines. Like the newlywed couple dancing on the hilltop, he knows in his very bones that it is a time to celebrate.

The time is the present. We are at the edge of the Cleveland National Forest in Riverside County, California, on ground once sacred to the Luiseno Indians. Four friends, two men and two women, have agreed to meet before dawn to climb into the hills to watch a December sunrise together.

By profession they are an architect, a massage therapist, a gardener, and a writer. All share a keen interest in ecological issues and a passion for life. During the years they've known each other, they've shared joys and sorrows, accomplishments and tragedies. Their friendship has served as an anchor of kindness and genuineness in the bizarre, stress-filled maelstrom that is life in the late twentieth century.

They stand in somewhat awkward silence, watching the eastern horizon. Their breath condenses in the chilly air. Birds in the canyon below begin to sing as the first ray of dawn pierces the horizon. The four join hands in a silent prayer for the Earth. As the Sun comes fully above the hills to the southeast and the air begins to warm, they lift their arms, turn clockwise, and begin a spontaneous circle dance. They move slowly at first, but the light in one another's eyes seems to propel them a little faster, then faster still, wheeling and kicking and jumping. By now all are laughing heartily and they break into a long, fond group hug. Smiling and still holding hands, they start back down the hillside. It is the winter Solstice.

For thousands of years our ancestors marked the seasons of the year with festivals. These festivals—of which the greatest and most universally observed were the twice-yearly Solstices—served many

5

functions. They bound together young and old, women and men, rich and poor. They gave people an emotional outlet and a break from ordinary cultural strictures and boundaries. All work was put aside; prisoners were freed; masters and servants traded places.

The festivals also provided ways for the community to govern itself. Not only did the people enjoy themselves on these occasions, but in gathering together they had opportunity to discuss their collective affairs. Politics and revelry were combined, for example, in the staging and acting out of plays satirizing unpopular nobles, merchants, and church officials.

But perhaps most importantly, the old seasonal festivals deepened people's sense of connection with land and sky. The Sun, Moon, stars, trees, crops, and animals were all included in the celebration. Each person felt a heightened connection with the Source of all life. In short, the festival was the community's way of renewing itself and its bonds with nature.

For the most part, we who live at the end of the twentieth century no longer celebrate these ancient festivals. Or, if we do, we observe them in unrecognizable forms—as (for example) in Christmas and New Year gatherings. But these are often highly commercialized affairs. Gone is the sense of participation in the cyclic interaction of the Earth and the heavens.

Now, we seem to be interested only in our human business. We rarely look up at the night sky, and we tend to observe a sunrise or sunset with only casual interest.

Meanwhile, human society creaks and groans under the weight of violence, injustice, overpopulation, poverty, and greed. And our ties with nature are strained nearly to the breaking point from water and air pollution, the destruction of the ozone layer, global warming, species extinctions, and deforestation.

Could there be a connection between our ignorance of the seasonal festivals and our loss of relatedness with one another and with the Earth?

These days, people everywhere are voicing their concerns about the environment and are looking for ways to make a difference.

More and more, we sense that it is time to return our attention to the Earth and to heal the rift we have created.

Perhaps it is time also to return to the festivals.

The recovery of the ancient seasonal festivals is more than a symbolic gesture. It can be a meaningful way of reminding ourselves of the natural order of things. It can also provide opportunities to increase our awareness of nature and to affirm our commitment to its welfare.

Seasonal festivals shouldn't be thought of merely as cultural relics. They were—and potentially *are*—joyous, fun, mischievous, profound, life-affirming events that connect us deeply with the land, the sky, and the wellspring of being within us.

Festivals are times of singing, dancing, and laughter. They are times when the child inside each of us is allowed to come out and play. They are times when old and young find a cross-generational bond. They are times when we return to the simple truths at the heart of life.

Is the celebration of the Solstices pagan or un-Christian? Certainly, the great seasonal festivals *were* key elements of the religions of pre-Christian Europe. But the Solstices themselves transcend religious ideology: they are simply astronomical facts. And they were celebrated by ancient peoples everywhere in the world, not just by the inhabitants of so-called pagan Europe.

Moreover, the early Christians were quick to appropriate the ancient festivals into their own calendar of holy days. As we see in Chapter 7, Christmas—the most popular Christian holiday— was deliberately timed to coincide with the winter Solstice. This is partly because the winter Solstice and Christmas are both times to celebrate the birth of light and to affirm our hope for the renewal of the world.

Many familiar Yuletide customs have more to do with the winter Solstice than with Christian doctrine. The mixture of the two celebrations at first served to popularize the Christian festival and later served to preserve some of the ancient Solstice traditions that were in danger of being forgotten.

But perhaps separating the two festivals once again—the Solstice on one hand, and Christmas on the other—will make it easier for Christians to refocus the unique meaning of their midwinter holiday and for us all to rediscover a celebration in which *everyone* can participate.

We can all benefit from attention paid to our home planet and to her relationship with the cosmos beyond. Whether we are Christians, Jews, Muslims, Hindus, Buddhists, followers of Native American or African religions, agnostics, or atheists, we can express our gratitude for the gifts of light and life. The Solstice isn't about worshipping particular gods or goddesses. It is about life itself.

This book is designed to help you and your family and friends engage in full-bodied, ecstatic seasonal renewal by recovering an experience that had deep meaning for the ancients and that is increasingly relevant today to a world on the edge of environmental catastrophe.

In Chapter 2, we see just what the Solstices and Equinoxes are, in simple astronomical terms. Then, in Chapters 3 through 8, we briefly survey the ways people have celebrated the Solstices—from the Paleolithic era to the present, and from Europe to China to pre-Columbian America.

In Chapter 9 we examine the intrinsic cultural and psychological meanings of the Solstices; and in Chapters 10 and 11 we explore ways you and your family and friends can celebrate the Solstice now—ways that will benefit both you and the planet. A festival is not an occasion for pious preaching, empty resolutions, or self-recrimination. It is an opportunity to enhance your experience of life in the eternal present. There's plenty of information in this book to satisfy your curiosity about the history, mythology, and meaning of the Solstices. But the real point of all of this information is to enable you to *celebrate now*.

CHAPTER 2

What Is a Solstice?

THE EARTH'S ROTATIONAL AXIS is not perpendicular to the plane of its orbit around the Sun. Instead, it is tilted at about 23½ degrees. It is this tilt that produces the seasons.

When the North Pole turns roughly in the direction of the Sun, it is summer in the northern hemisphere. The Sun is then more nearly overhead at noon, and so its rays strike the Earth at an angle that is closer to perpendicular. The days are long, and the nights short. Meanwhile, it is winter in the southern hemisphere, where the solar rays are more oblique; there the days are shorter, and the Sun is closer to the horizon all day long.

In six months, the situation will be reversed: the southern hemisphere will enjoy the long days and intense sunlight of summer, while the northern hemisphere will experience the dark, cold, gestative season of winter.

On two days a year, one in late December and the other in late June, the Earth's axis is tilted the most directly toward (and away from) the Sun that it will be during the year. On about June 21, when the North Pole is pointed Sunward, people in the northern

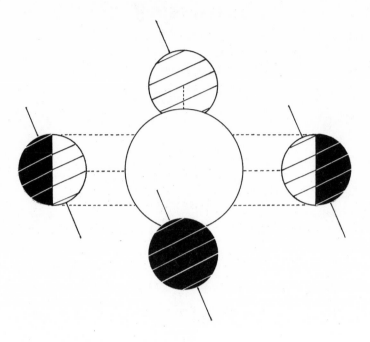

The Earth in relation to the Sun at the Solstices (left and right) and Equinoxes (above and below). The latitudinal lines around the Earth are the Arctic Circle, the Tropic of Cancer, the equator, Tropic of Capricorn, and the Antarctic Circle. For observers at the Tropics of Cancer and Capricorn, the Sun is directly overhead—at the zenith—at noon on the summer Solstice (late June in the north, late December in the south). For an observer at the Arctic or Antarctic circles, the Sun stays just above the horizon at midnight on the summer Solstice, and never quite rises on the winter Solstice.

hemisphere experience the longest day and the shortest night of the year. This is their summer Solstice. For people in the southern hemisphere, the same day is their winter Solstice.

Six months later, the Earth has traveled halfway along its yearly solar orbit. Now the South Pole is turned as far in the direction of the Sun as it will get during the year. It is winter Solstice in Europe and North America, but it is summer Solstice in southern Africa and South America, and in Australia and New Zealand.

The word *Solstice* comes from the Latin words *Sol stetit*, which mean, literally, "the Sun stood still." From the observer's point of view on Earth's northern hemisphere, the Sun rises and sets further south on the horizon as winter Solstice approaches; it rises and sets further north as summer Solstice nears (the situation being reversed in the southern hemisphere). The movement of the points of solar rising and setting along the eastern and western horizons quickens in spring and autumn but slows as the Solstices approach. Then, for about six days in late December and again in late June, the Sun appears to rise and set at almost exactly the same places. Its rising and setting points appear to stand still—hence the name *Solstice*.

The Solstices divide the year into two halves—six months of waxing Sun, followed by six months of waning Sun. These two half-yearly sub-cycles constitute a pair of complementary opposites—like day and night, light and dark, heat and cold, positive and negative. Ancient peoples knew that everything needs an opposite or complement to give it meaning and vitality. It is the interplay of complementary principles that gives rise to movement and change.

But the points of division—the boundaries or edges between complements—are ambiguous, neither this nor that. They are mysterious and magical, belonging to neither this world nor the next, and therefore serve as gateways between dimensions, realities, and states of consciousness. This is why the Solstices, as hinges of the seasons, were always regarded as times when the two worlds were especially close. They were times of danger and opportunity; times for special alertness and aliveness.

Equinoxes and Quarter Days

Halfway between the Solstices, in late March and again in late September, there are two days when the northern and southern hemispheres receive the same amount of sunlight and the days and nights are of the same length. Then, the tilt of Earth's axis is not toward the Sun, but lies at a right angle to an imaginary Earth-Sun line. At the equator, the Sun is directly overhead. These days

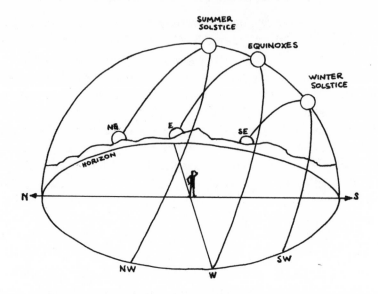

In the northern temperate zone, an observer sees the Sun at the summer solstice rise in the northeast and pass high overhead at noon. The winter Solstice Sun rises to the southeast and remains low in the sky all day.

are the Equinoxes (*Equinox* means "equal night"). Ancient peoples regarded the Equinoxes, like the Solstices, as significant moments of the year, nodes in the yearly cycle of seasons.

The Equinoxes are times of balance, and yet they are also times of intense change: the solar rising and setting points are moving quickly from day to day—southward during autumn, northward during spring. For most ancient peoples, the spring—or *vernal*—Equinox was always celebrated as a time of new life, while the fall Equinox was naturally a harvest festival.

In Celtic Europe there were other seasonal festivals as well—the quarter days, so called because they fall midway between Solstice and Equinox.

Imbolg (from the Celtic word for "sheep's milk"), falling on February 2, was the start of the lambing season. Also called *Brigid* or (in the Christian calendar) *Candlemas*, it marks the return of the light, a station in the yearly process of transformation from inner,

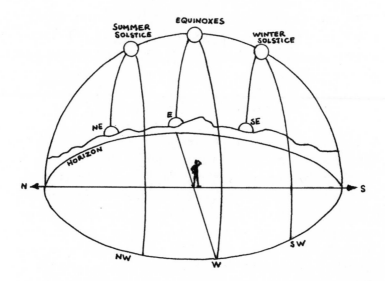

For an observer at the equator, the Sun passes through the zenith at noon on the Equinoxes.

contemplative focus toward outer manifestation. Imbolg survives in modern America as Groundhog Day.

Beltane (or *Beltine*), the first day of May, was celebrated with great bonfires in Scotland, Wales, Sweden, and Bohemia. The dance around the Maypole and the selection of a king and queen of the May are rites that have continued in Europe into modern times. The eve of May Day is *Walpurgis Nacht*, when witches were supposed to ride through the night sky on hellish missions.

Lughnasad (called *Lammas* in England), which falls on August 1, is the festival of the first fruits. It was celebrated in Ireland by digging up the first potatoes of the new crop. Formerly the observance included cheerful gatherings on hilltops, dancing, wooing, and the picking of wildflowers as well.

Samhain (pronounced sah-win and meaning "summer's end," and also known as *All Hallows Eve* or *Hallowe'en*) originally fell in early November, but was later observed on October 31. The ancient Celtic peoples celebrated Samhain as their New Year. Like the other quarter days, it is an occasion when the world of spirits was thought to be closer than usual to the human world. This brought inspiration and renewal, but danger as well. Therefore Samhain (and Hallowe'en) celebrations served largely to hold evil entities at bay.

The Precession of the Equinoxes

The direction of Earth's axis of rotation remains relatively constant as the planet pursues its yearly orbit around the Sun. That is, the north pole points continually in one direction.

But the direction of the axis does change a little, though very slowly, tracing a circle through the heavens once every twenty-six thousand years. If you imagine a child's whirling top in place of the Earth, this motion of the axis—called *precession* by astronomers—is equivalent to the wobble the top develops as it slows down.

Today, when we in the northern hemisphere look up at the night sky, the starry vault seems to rotate slowly around Polaris, the pole star. But because of the slow precessional motion of the Earth's axis, Polaris will eventually be replaced by a new pole star. In the distant past, there were other pole stars before Polaris, and there were also long periods of time when there was no pole star and the axis pointed toward empty space.

Many ancient peoples were fascinated by this precessional motion and (according to Giorgio de Santillana and Hertha von Dechend in their classic study, *Hamlet's Mill*) made it the centerpiece of many of their myths. This is remarkable, because the ancients could only have become aware of the precessional motion of the axis by performing astronomical observations continuously for many centuries and keeping close track of what they saw. (It is worth noting, though, that most conventional astronomers ascribe the discovery of the precession to the Greek philosopher-scientist Hipparchos around 130 B.C.E., and tend to discount Santillana's and von Dechend's arguments.)

As every astrologer knows, the zodiac is a band of constellations in roughly the same plane as our solar orbit. Throughout the year, as the Earth orbits the Sun, the latter appears (from Earth) to

The precessional "wobble" of the Earth's axis takes about twenty-six thousand years to complete one cycle.

move through one of these constellations after another, at the rate of about one every month. At night, the planets (which are also roughly in the plane of the Earth's orbit) can likewise be plotted by their proximity to the various zodiacal constellations.

Because of the precessional motion of the Earth's axis, however, each time the Earth returns to a particular place in its orbit (the vernal Equinox, for example), its axis is pointing at a slightly different place in the sky, and the Sun, therefore, occupies a slightly different place in relation to the zodiac. It is a subtle change, but it adds up. Because of it, every twenty-one hundred years, the Equinox Sun appears in front of a new zodiacal constellation. Today, the Sun appears in Pisces at the vernal Equinox. About two thousand years ago it occupied the sign of Aries, the ram. Ahead is the age of Aquarius, the water bearer. And twenty-six thousand years from now, the Sun at spring Equinox will appear in precisely the same position in relation to zodiac as it does now—though by then the stars in many familiar constellations will have shifted position noticeably.

In addition to the precessional motion of the terrestrial axis, the ancients knew about the zodiac as well, and over the course of several millennia, they watched the Sun at the vernal Equinox appearing in one constellation after another. They regarded this motion from one star cluster to the next as the end of one world age and the beginning of the next.

The ancients were obviously keen observers of the night sky. Yet they had no telescopes or other complicated instruments. Their primary observational technique consisted simply of watching and recording the rising and setting points of various celestial objects over long periods of time. For people so attuned to cosmic rhythms, the Solstices and Equinoxes had a significance we can barely imagine—a significance they commemorated in a myriad of ways.

PART TWO

The Solstice Tradition

To every thing there is a season, and a time to every purpose
under heaven:

A time to be born, and a time to die; a time to plant and a time
to pluck up that which is planted;

A time to kill, and a time to heal; a time to break down, and
a time to build up;

A time to weep, and a time to laugh; a time to mourn, and a
time to dance;

A time to cast away stones and a time to gather stones together;
a time to embrace, and a time to refrain from embracing;

A time to get, and a time to lose; a time to keep and a time to
cast away;

A time to rend, and a time to sew; a time to keep silence, and
a time to speak;

A time to love, and a time to hate; a time of war, and a time
of peace.

—Ecclesiastes 3:1–8

CHAPTER 3

The First Solstice Festivals

THE VERY EARLIEST SYMBOLS that Ice Age people carved in bone and mammoth tusk were records of celestial cycles. If our oldest persistent concerns are also our deepest, then it follows that one of our most powerful needs as humans must be to observe and conform with the rhythms of nature and cosmos.

This should not be surprising. Nature is a temporal mesh of thousands of interlocked cycles, and we, after all, are a part of nature.

Virtually all plants and animals follow an innate twenty-four-hour (or circadian, from the Latin *circa dies*, "about a day") cycle of activity. Some obey tidal, lunar, and circannual (yearly) internal clocks as well. These biological rhythms are so deeply embedded in organisms that even individual cells raise and lower their metabolic activity in a daily beat. And many biological clocks keep time in the absence of external cues, such as the presence or absence of sunlight. For example, in a 1963 experiment, a Rocky Mountain ground squirrel was kept for a year in a small windowless room with artificial light, and sufficient food and water. The room's temperature was maintained at a constant zero degrees Celsius.

From August to October, the squirrel sustained a constant body temperature of thirty-seven degrees and ate normally. But in October, the animal stopped eating and went into hibernation, just as it would have in the wild. Five months later, it came out of hibernation and began feeding normally.

According to Frank Brown of Northwestern University, who performed dozens of experiments in the 1950s and 60s having to do with biological rhythms, living things keep their clocks synchronized at least in part through sensitivity to minute magnetic and electrical fields in the Earth—fields that shift and change with our planet's daily and yearly cycles and according to the positions of Sun and Moon.[1]

Our own bodies are governed by dozens of such cycles. Our body temperature and skin temperature rise and fall by a degree or two on a circadian schedule. Most people's favorite time of day coincides with the hours of maximum body heat—typically, the afternoon or early evening. The time of peak excretion of adrenal steroids follows the same rhythm and peaks at the same time as the body-temperature cycle. The speed of blood coagulation, white blood-cell count, glycogen production by the liver, protein utilization in metabolism, EEG rhythms, heart rate, respiratory rate, and many other biological functions also maintain a regular, twenty-four-hour beat. As anyone who has experienced jet lag or worked a night shift knows, circadian rhythms are powerful, and any effort to change them can result in swings of mood, loss of appetite, gastrointestinal distress, decrease in attention span and alertness, inability to sleep, and general fatigue.[2]

Many of these daily internal cycles are coordinated by the pineal gland with the longer, seasonal rhythms of the Sun. As the days shorten, the pineal secretes more melatonin, a hormone that controls the amount of serotonin in the brain, regulates sexual function, and (when significantly elevated over a period of weeks) triggers moods of depression. As the days lengthen, the process reverses. This explains the well-known pattern of winter depression followed by "spring fever," which occurs more noticeably in latitudes far from the equator, where winter days are shortest. Seasonal variations have also been observed in suicide rates and in illnesses such as ulcers and psychoses, which may be tied to the mood-altering effects of melatonin. The pineal, whose function is still poorly understood, is photo-sensitive and, through its influence on the rest of the endocrine system, seems to act as a coupling mechanism to keep the body "in tune" with its environment (biological rhythm researcher Gay Gaer Luce says its purpose is to "maintain phase relationships in a multi-oscillator system"). This function of mediating the cycles of Heaven and Earth, so to speak, perhaps accounts for some of the mystical beliefs that have surrounded this tiny gland in cultures around the world.[3]

Researchers have observed even more seasonal periodicities in animals than in humans. Dutch and German scientists have shown that there is a seasonal difference in the amount of glycogen stored in animal liver cells. In rodents, the amount of liver glycogen found in January was double that in July. And Dr. H. von Mayersbach of Hanover, Germany, while tracking DNA and RNA rhythms in liver tissue in laboratory animals, found subtle but pronounced changes in tissue structure with seasonal change.[4] But more obviously, animals show highly specific seasonal patterns of mating, hibernation, and migration. While migratory paths in many animals seem to be mapped according to the geomagnetic field, the *timing* of hibernation, mating, and migration have been shown to be tied to seasonal variations in sunlight.[5]

Of course, humans do not apparently migrate, mate, or hibernate according to a strict seasonal schedule. Much that is instinctual in animals is culturally orchestrated in humans. Social rhythms bind individuals to cultures, and cultures to nature. As an example, consider the seasonal migrations of the Aboriginal Australians, who followed the same invisible paths across the land for untold generations—paths which they memorized and communicated through a series of songs. From a purely economic point of view, they were merely following the seasonally available food supply. But they believed that their songs were essential to the periodic revitalization—even re-*creation*—of plants and animals, hills and streams. While to an outsider their land would appear utterly trackless, the Aboriginals knew it in exhaustive detail and regarded themselves as its divinely empowered keepers. Their *corroborees*—

ceremonies in which the primordial acts of creation on the part of mythic ancestral beings were sung and danced in the eternal present—punctuated the year in such a way as to weave together individual human cycles of maturation (for these were occasions for puberty and other initiatory rites); the migratory cycles of animals; and the times of the propagation and ripening of wild food plants.

Every culture has its own rhythm with its own speed and its own temporal cues. Indeed, culture can be defined in part as a condition of temporal entrainment in which rituals, calendars, and (in more modern societies) clocks and computers are used to join individuals and families into a larger functional unit.

In sum, we are discovering that, as Jeremy Rifkin writes in his book *Time Wars*,

> temporal considerations play an essential role in ordering the entire life process. Below material surfaces, life is animated and structured by an elaborate set of intricately synchronized rhythms that parallel the frequencies of the larger universe. Chronobiology provides a rich new conceptual framework for rethinking the notion of relationships in nature. In the temporal scheme of things, life, earth, and universe are viewed as partners in a tightly synchronized dance in which all of the separate movements pulse in unison to create a single organic whole.[6]

Today, however, we human beings have created a situation unique in nature, as well as in the history of our own species. We have gradually but decisively cut ourselves off from many of the cycles of the cosmos and of the biosphere and substituted arbitrary, economically determined temporal patterns. We have overridden the natural daily rhythms of light and dark with the artificial illumination of cities; the rhythms of the seasons with greenhouses and supermarkets, jet travel and central heating. Electromagnetic fields from power lines, house wiring, and appliances drown out subtle geomagnetic signals from the Earth. Clock time has replaced Sun and Moon time; nanosecond computer time makes heartbeat time imprecise and irrelevant.

22

We are paying a price for this temporal revolution—a cost of stress and disease that only masks the deeper sacrifice of our sense of belonging, of being contained within a context that transcends human political and economic systems, of being nurtured by the heartbeat of creation.

It may be an uncommon act of sanity, therefore, to pause in our headlong rush toward speed and efficiency to recall how our ancestors, rather than suppressing or manipulating natural cycles, survived by being sensitive to them and harmonizing their lives with them.

Paleolithic and Neolithic Europe

Human beings have existed in more or less their present an-atomical form for tens of thousands of years—exactly how long is debatable. While they used stone tools from the earliest times, there is no evidence of symbolic expression until about thirty thousand years ago, when our ancestors of the Paleolithic, or Old Stone Age, began scratching tally marks on bone and ivory to record the phases of the Moon. At first, the scientists who found examples of these marks assumed that they were mere decoration or hunting tallies. But in the 1960s, archaeologist Alexander Marshack examined all of the known specimens under a microscope and found that the marks follow a pattern that corresponds to the lunar cycle. While these twenty- to thirty-thousand-year-old notations offer no specific evidence that people then were also aware of the Solstices, they nevertheless show a concern for the passage of time, and for celes-tial cycles. The later Paleolithic paintings in the caves of south-western Europe depict seasonal events—molting bison, a pregnant mare, mating snakes. According to archaeoastronomer E. C. Krupp, these paintings reveal concerns similar to those that motivate contemporary shamanic peoples to make calendars in order to limit hunting to certain seasons, ensuring the survival of game species.[7]

In short, while we know little about their specific religious beliefs and seasonal observances, we do know that the people of the Old Stone Age were vitally concerned with the rhythms of Earth and sky.

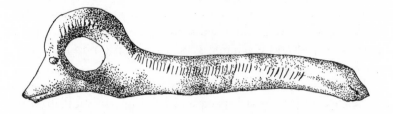

The Smiling Fox bâton from Le Placard, Charente, France. Dating from about twenty thousand years ago, during the last Ice Age, this carved antler displays a typical sequence of notches on both sides and on the "belly" as well. It is about a foot in length. (After Hadingham)

By the time of the New Stone Age, however, some six to eight thousand years ago, there are plenty of signs that seasonal festivals were at the center of community life. People were, by this time, organized into tribes, the members of which could trace common ancestral origins, and whose territories were bounded by natural features of the land—rivers, mountains, and forests. Each tribe had a unique dialect and common religious ideas and rites. The land itself was held jointly. As individual tribes grew too populous for local resources, they would divide into two or more kinship groups, each consisting of people who could trace their lineage to a common ancestress—the woman around whose family the clan was created.

But as their population increased, the people were forced to restrict their migrations; they settled and began to supplement hunting and gathering with horticulture. Towns appeared and classes emerged within society—chiefs, priests, warriors, artisans, and peasants. Most groups lived close to rivers or to the sea, and most trade and travel were by water. Gradually, small, local groups bound themselves together into larger political, economic, and cultural units with shared language and customs. Periodic festivals supplied much of the cohesive force that joined clan with clan. These Neolithic farmers and seafarers, whose lives so utterly depended on the weather and the seasons, naturally chose to come together

The entrance to Newgrange. Above the doorway is the lightbox; before it sits a carved boulder.

at regular intervals to direct their appeals to the energies they believed must control the basic cycle of nature—birth, life, death, and rebirth—in which crops, animals, and humans all participate.

The View from Earth's Womb

Beginning perhaps eleven millennia ago, the Neolithic Europeans began to erect ceremonial structures to assist in attuning themselves to, and manipulating, these energies. This was the megalithic age—from the Greek words *mega*, meaning "big," and *lithos*, meaning "stone." The earliest of the megaliths seem to have been constructed by pre-Indo-European peoples, a maritime, matriarchal, map-making culture of small, long-headed people called the *Priteni* (the source for the names *Britain* and *Brittany*).[8] The Priteni were displaced, beginning about 2800 B.C.E., by the round-headed Beaker People, so called because of their practice of burying an elaborate clay cup or beaker with their dead. These and other subsequent invaders seem to have taken over the megalithic sites and used them for their own purposes—often as tombs.

Twenty-eight miles north of Dublin, Ireland, on a ridge over-looking the river Boyne, stands a magnificent womb-shaped passage chamber composed of hundreds of selected glacial boulders, roofed with great corbeled slabs, and covered by an immense mound comprised of neat layers of turf and water-rolled pebbles. Its facade is gleaming quartz. Its roof slabs incorporate carved drainage channels to keep rainwater from entering the interior, which consists of a sixty-two-foot corridor ending in a twenty-foot-high vaulted chamber surrounded by three small rooms, each with a basin stone. Newgrange, as the chamber has been called in recent times, was built around 3350 B.C.E., eight hundred years before the first Egyptian pyramid. It was, in the words of its restorers, archaeologists Michael and Claire O'Kelly, "no trial-and-error, hit-and-miss affair, but the work of practised builders who fully appreciated the factors which would best assure long life for their monument."[9]

Each year, for about a week before and after the winter Solstice, light from the rising Sun passes through a boxed slot above the doorway of Newgrange and shines the entire length of the corridor to the far wall of the central chamber (a distance of over eighty feet), illuminating a stone basin positioned below a series of intricate carvings of interlocked spirals, eye shapes, and rayed solar discs. For about seventeen minutes the inner sanctuary is softly lit; then the finger of sunlight slowly creeps back across the stone floor, and darkness returns. The effect is stunning, and the effort spent to obtain it must have been enormous.

Why did the people who built Newgrange go to so much trouble? If they had meant the structure as a tomb, they could have achieved their purpose with far less work. Its construction required the prolonged labor of an extensive community; to achieve the lighting effect in the interior, precise measurements were required. In order to justify such an effort it must have served some purpose vital to generations of people throughout a considerable geographical area. Since the structure is clearly designed to come alive at one specific time of the year—the winter Solstice—the impressiveness of the engineering and sheer size of Newgrange give us some idea of the importance which the Neolithic farmers of Ireland must have placed in that yearly event. Lacking written

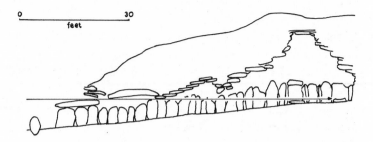

The upward sloping floor of Newgrange keeps sunlight from penetrating more than a few feet into the interior of the structure. But the roofbox above the door permits the winter solstice Sun to shine to the far end of the passage.

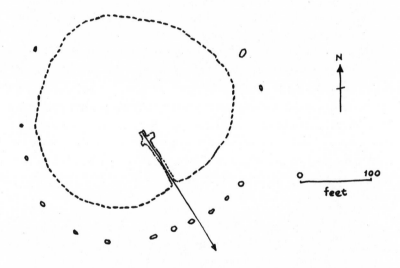

The plan of Newgrange, showing the winter Solstice alignment. (After Krupp)

records, we cannot know precisely what they did, thought, and felt on those prehistoric December mornings as sunlight penetrated the sacred, symbolic womb they had built. But the human remains that have been discovered in the side chambers suggest that the place must have served as a temple for the contemplation of the mysteries of birth and death and the connection between the human soul and the cycles of the cosmos.

Perhaps the significance of the place lies not in the *idea* of commemorating either an astronomical phenomenon or a deceased matriarch, but rather in the *experience* the structure elicits in the human psyche. It is an effect that makes the relationships between the Sun and the Earth, life and death—relationships which we modern people tend to think of in abstract terms—viscerally sensible.

Of course, we can only speculate about what people actually *did* on those cold December mornings. It seems likely that many thousands of people would have gathered and camped, probably for a period of several days. These must have been times of playing and feasting, and of conducting political and economic business as well. Since the inner chambers of Newgrange are only large enough to accommodate a few people, the ceremonies themselves must have been led by one or several priests or priestesses, with everyone else observing, dancing, chanting, and praying around the periphery of the structure.

Some lesser-known but older passage chambers are to be found about forty miles from Newgrange, in the Loughcrew Mountains. In his book *The Stars and the Stones*, art historian Martin Brennan tells of his impressions at the spring Equinox sunrise inside Cairn T, the highest and most central of the mounds:

> On the upper left of the backstone a rectangular patch of light was rapidly beginning to take form, brilliantly illuminating the entire chamber in a glowing splendour of shimmering golden orange light. It was dazzling, and when we entered the chamber we stood back and gazed in awe. Naturally, we had expected to see something similar to what we had seen at Newgrange. There, the low angle of the sun rising at winter solstice causes the beam of light to sweep across the chamber. Here, however, the light assumed a clearly defined geometric shape that was projected on to the upright backstone and moved diagonally across it, tracing the path of the sun against a mural of prehistoric

art. What impressed us most was the careful and delicate modelling of the light beam by the huge stones forming the passage chamber, and how the shape of the beam conformed to the patterns engraved on the stone. For the first time we were seeing the signs and symbols in the context in which the artist had meant them to be seen. Suddenly markings that had appeared to be random and haphazard became part of an intricately structured system that derived its meaning from the solar event we were witnessing.[10]

Hundreds of similar mounds, barrows, quoits, and passage chambers dotted megalithic Europe. And many (though not all) appear to have been oriented toward sunrise or sunset on the Solstices or Equinoxes. Apparently the Moon's movements were accorded an equal religious importance. The most richly carved chambered passage mound in Europe, at Gavrinis in Brittany, is aligned to the southernmost moonrise. The same alignment is found in stone circles in northeast Scotland. Moreover, it seems that some of the megalithic sites were intended as temples of *both* the Sun and the Moon. At Cairn T at Loughcrew, for example, Martin Brennan observed lunar as well as solar light phenomena. And while Gavrinis, like Newgrange, receives the light of the Midwinter sunrise, a stone of white quartz situated halfway along its passage appears to have been intended to reflect the light of both the Sun and Moon.

As William H. Calvin has shown in his book *How the Shaman Stole the Moon*, ancient peoples learned to predict eclipses by studying the rising points of both Sun and Moon. When both rose and set at the same points on the horizon and the Moon was dark, a solar eclipse was possible; if the Moon was full, a lunar eclipse was likely.

The Priteni seem to have associated the Sun, Moon, and Earth with the Goddess. These earliest megalith builders apparently kept a solar calendar of eight or sixteen divisions, and could in principle have used places like Newgrange as observatories to determine the approximate size of the planet, and the length of the year to within a minute.

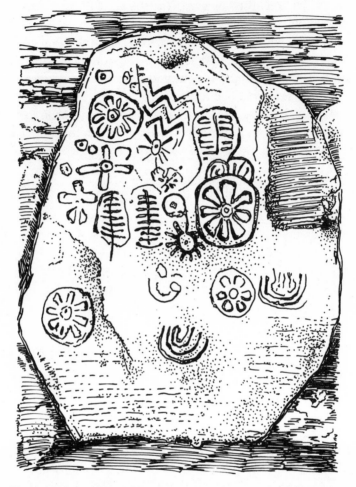

The backstone of Cairn T, Loughcrew, which is lit by the Equinox sunrise. (After Michell)

Rings of Stone

Ancient peoples used four primary ways of marking the Solstices and Equinoxes. The first involved the creation of spotlighting effects on the walls of passage chambers (as at Newgrange), or caves (as in the case of the Chumash shamans of California, whom we consider in Chapter 5). Peoples who favored this method often carved or painted symbols where they would be struck by a beam of light at sunrise or sunset on one of the Solstices or Equinoxes.

A second method involved measuring the shadow of an upright pillar, or *gnomon*—usually at noon. In the temperate zones, the shadow is shortest at the summer Solstice, longest in midwinter. This was the technique of choice of the Babylonians, Ionian Greeks, Chinese, and Peruvians, as it still is among some modern Borneo tribes.

Another zenith-based system, used by many Central and South American tribes, required a specially-prepared ceremonial structure. Only at noon on the longest day of the year would the Sun shine directly through a hole or tube in its ceiling and onto a particular spot on the floor.

The fourth and simplest way to mark the Solstices was to watch, from a fixed position, where on the horizon the Sun rose and set over a period of years. As we have already noted, the southern- and northernmost sunrise and sunset points correspond with the winter and summer Solstices. The use of this last method was widespread throughout Europe, Asia, and the Americas.

Stonehenge, on the Wiltshire plain of southwest England, incorporated this last method. If one stands at the center of the monument and faces northeast along its axis, the isolated thirty-five-ton Heel Stone appears 256 feet away between three of the great stone arches, marking the approximate place on the horizon of the summer Solstice sunrise. The Heel Stone is somewhat offset from the actual point of sunrise, however; it is the structure's overall axis that is accurately aligned to the Solstice. In recent years, astronomers and archaeologists have discovered at least two dozen other solar and lunar alignments the ancient builders of Stonehenge incorporated into the structure. While many of these alignments have been disputed, it is clear that, in the words of astronomer E. C. Krupp, "we need no longer doubt whether Stonehenge had astronomical significance. Instead, we might marvel that it had so much significance."[11]

The summer Solstice alignment at Stonehenge. (After Hadingham)

A reconstruction of Stonehenge III.

The most impressive and famous of Great Britain's nine hundred Neolithic stone circles, Stonehenge was built over a period of many centuries, from around 2800 B.C.E., not by Celtic Druids, as was once thought, but by pre-Celtic peoples, beginning (perhaps) with the Priteni. Its sarsen stones, which weigh up to fifty tons each, were quarried twenty miles to the north in Marlborough Downs;

the bluestones came from much further away in Wales. While the monument's later additions and alterations (which archaeologists designate as Stonehenge II and III) changed the appearance of the structure drastically, most of the astronomical alignments are embodied in the original plan.

We can only imagine the uses to which Stonehenge was actually put. At the summer Solstice, it must have been a gathering place for tribes from throughout southern England. At night, fires must have lit the upright pillars, throwing them into stark relief against the night sky. Perhaps great circle or spiral dances were held throughout the night around and among the stone rings. Then, at sunrise, all eyes must have focused on the priests and priestesses marking the alignment from the center of Stonehenge to the Heel Stone.

Today, Stonehenge is one of England's premier tourist attractions, seen by some seven hundred thousand people annually. Visitors are prevented from entering the rings of stones; instead, they are funnelled from the nearby car park along a paved path that curves halfway around the sarsen circle. While this is necessary to the preservation of the site, the nearby motorway, the chain-link fence, the guards, the sidewalk, and the tourists all conspire to undermine its impressiveness and sacredness. Still, as one drives west on A303 from Amesbury, Stonehenge announces itself on the western horizon like an unexpected message from home. With the great upright monoliths in view, the surrounding cars, roads, and utility lines look somehow alien and fleeting.

Woodhenge, a short drive east from Stonehenge, is a set of six concentric ovals of postholes, now filled with concrete markers. It was built at about the same time as Stonehenge I, and its main axis is oriented to sunrise on the summer Solstice.

Other stone circles or groups of standing stones whose alignments include dates from the solar calendar include Maes Howe in the Scottish Orkney Islands, oriented to Midwinter sunset; Kintraw in Argyll, Scotland, also oriented to Midwinter sunset; Ballochroy, on the Kintyre peninsula of Scotland, which incorporates sunset alignments at both summer and winter Solstice; Long Meg and Her Daughters, in Cumberland, which indicates the winter

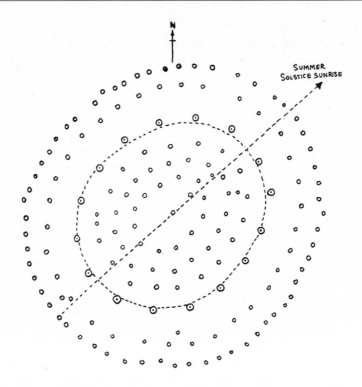

Plan of Woodhenge, showing the direction to summer Solstice sunrise.

Solstice sunset; Gors Fawr in southern Wales, which targets the summer Solstice sunrise; and Castle Rigg, in Cumbria, which includes summer Solstice sunset, winter Solstice sunrise, and Equinox sunrise alignments.

CHAPTER 4

Celebrations of Sun and Earth in the Ancient Near East

The IMPRESSIVE PHENOMENON of ancient Egyptian civilization—with its advanced medicine, engineering, mathematics, and astronomy—sprang into being virtually full-blown. Archaeologists are predisposed to explain this cultural explosion in the Nile valley some four-and-a-half thousand years ago as the result of a long period of development, or of influence from other, older centers of civilization. But these explanations never quite succeed. Any visit to a good collection of Egyptian artifacts, as at the British Museum, or even an hour with a book of photographs of pyramids and temples leaves the distinct impression that the earliest hieroglyphics, paintings, sculptures, and buildings of the Old Kingdom represented by far the clearest expression and fullest flowering of the Egyptian genius. All that came later, through nearly three millennia of pharaonic history, seems to have derived merely from the imitation and repetition of elements contained in an initial burst of inspiration.

While our understanding of ancient Egyptian society is still imperfect, nearly every scholar who has studied it has come to the conclusion that religion and magic formed its entire basis.

The Egyptians were preoccupied with the meaning of life and death, with religious symbolism of all kinds, with astronomy, and with the principles of harmony and proportion as applied to the interconnected cycles of the cosmic, human, natural, and supernatural worlds.

To the Egyptians, the Sun was Re, the chief of the gods, who created the world and governed it during the First Time, a Golden Age of peace and plenty. Amenhotep IV, the heretical pharaoh of the Eighteenth Dynasty, made the Sun the *only* god, which he worshiped as *Aton*—an Egyptian word that referred to the physical disk of the Sun (the other solar names *Re*, *Atum*, *Horus*, and *Amun*, in contrast, had mythological associations). He called himself Akhenaton ("The Glory of Aton"), and moved the capital of Egypt from Thebes to a new city, built in the center of the country, which he called Akhetaton. He forbade the artistic representation of other deities, and no images of Aton were allowed save that of the solar disk with its rays outstretched toward Earth, each ending with a hand proffering the symbol for life. In a Hymn to Aton by Akhenaton or his royal poet, found inscribed on a mausoleum for the father of Nefertiti, the Pharaoh's wife, we read:

Thou dost appear beautiful on the horizon of heaven,
  O living Aton, thou who wast the first to live.
When thou hast risen on the eastern horizon,
  Thou hast filled every land with thy beauty. . . .
When thou dost set on the western horizon,
  The earth is in darkness, resembling death. . . .
At daybreak, when thou dost rise on the horizon,
  Dost shine as Aton by day,
Thou dost dispel the darkness
  And shed thy rays.
The two lands are in a festive mood,
  Awake, and stand on their feet,
For thou hast raised them up;
  They cleanse their bodies and take their garments;
  Their arms are lifted in adoration at thine appearing;
  The whole land performs its labor.

All beasts are satisfied with their pasture;
   Trees and plants are verdant.
The birds which fly from their nests, their wings are spread
   in adoration to thy soul. . . .

Akhenaton, who added to his name the phrase "Living in Truth," encouraged the artists of the new royal city to paint in a naturalistic style and did away with the severe etiquette traditional to the royal household. But his reform was widely opposed and ended with his death. His works were obliterated, and later generations of Egyptians regarded him with contempt. His son and successor Tutankhamen reinstated the theocracy of the Theban priesthood, but died before reaching the age of twenty. Soon afterward the Eighteenth Dynasty ended in chaos, and with it passed the last great flowering of the Egyptian genius.

For a people who worshiped the Sun, both as a mythological idea and as an all-important daily celestial phenomenon, the Solstices and Equinoxes must have appeared as divinely ordained temporal thresholds. And, as the Egyptians' astronomy was focused on the eastern horizon, they aligned many of their temples to Solstice and Equinox sunrise points.

We can perhaps best appreciate the Egyptian worldview as it is reflected in architecture. As an example, the Temple of Amen-Ra at Karnak is, according to Sir J. Norman Lockyer, the great nineteenth-century pioneer of the science of archaeoastronomy, "beyond all question the most majestic ruin in the world." It was rebuilt by Pharaoh Thutmose III of the Eighteenth Dynasty, whose period (about 1480 B.C.E., in the early phase of the New Kingdom) represented the last flourishing of design and construction before the gradual decline of the Egyptian civilization. Parts of Karnak seem to be much older, however, dating perhaps to the Eleventh or Twelfth Dynasties of the Middle Kingdom. On the basis of astronomical considerations, Lockyer proposed that the foundations of the shrine must have been laid in the year 3700 B.C.E., or nearly a millennium before the building of the Old Kingdom pyramids—a date with which few modern Egyptologists would agree.

View along the Peristyle Hall of the Great Temple of Amen-Ra at Karnak.

What is beyond question, though, is that the Great Temple at Karnak incorporates Solstice alignments. Lockyer proposed that the main hall is oriented to the summer Solstice sunset. "There is a sort of stone avenue in the centre," he wrote,

> giving a view towards the north-west, and this axis is something like five hundred yards in length. The whole object of the builder of the great temple at Karnak—one of the most soul-stirring temples which have ever been conceived or built by man—was to preserve that axis absolutely open; and all the wonderful halls of columns and the like, as seen on one side or other of the axis, are merely details;

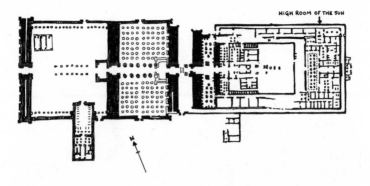

HIGH ROOM OF THE SUN

Plan of the Great Temple at Karnak.

the point being that the axis should be absolutely open, straight, and true.[1]

On the day of the Solstice, according to Lockyer, a beam of light would illuminate a sanctuary in the interior of the temple for no more than two or three minutes, during which time there would be an observable peak of brightness. This dramatic spotlighting effect would have allowed the Egyptian priests to determine the length of the solar year to within a minute.

The lighting effect would also have served religious purposes. Lockyer notes that "the most solemn ceremonial . . . in the whole year was that which took place on New Year's morning, or the great festival of the Nile-rising and summer Solstice, the 1st of Thoth."[2] This solstitial celebration "not only dominated the industry, but the astronomy and religion of Egypt. . . ."[3] In solemn processions, priests carried statues of Hapi—the god of the Nile—through the streets of towns and villages. Then, according to Egyptologist E. A. Wallis Budge, "When the inundation was abundant the rejoicings which took place after the performance of the religious ceremonies . . . were carried out on a scale of great magnificence, and all classes kept holiday."[4]

The axis of the smaller Temple of Ra-Hor-Ahkty, attached to the great hall at Karnak, is oriented to sunrise on the winter Solstice, as is the window of the High Room of the Sun in the same

The rooftop temple at Karnak known as the High Room of the Sun.

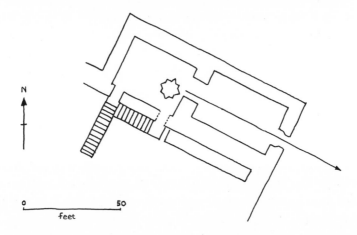

Plan of the small High Room of the Sun, showing the window opening to the winter Solstice sunrise.

temple complex. The Temples of Thebes and Abydos are similarly oriented, and so also the sixty-foot-high Colossi of Memnon on the plain on the other side of the Nile from Karnak, along with (probably) their associated ruined temple.

The Pyramids and the Sphinx at Gizeh, and their surrounding temples (the Temples of Isis and of Osiris), on the other hand, are oriented east-west, toward the Equinox sunrise. The same is true of the pyramids at Memphis, Sais and Tanis.

The ancient Egyptians possessed a genius for making the maximum use of the simplest principles and tools, both in engineering and in theoretical science. And it seems that it was through the astute use of their temple-observatories that they became aware of the slow precessional motion of the Earth's axis. Giorgio de Santillana of MIT has written that "when a stellar temple is oriented so accurately that it requires several reconstructions at intervals of a few centuries, which involve each time the rebuilding of its narrow alignment," as was true of Egyptian structures oriented to the rising of certain bright stars, and when these rebuildings are dated not with hieroglyphs representing years in relation to political events but by bas-relief zodiacs showing the position of the constellations (as is the case at the Temple of Hathor at Dendera), "then it is not reasonable to suppose the Egyptians unaware of the Precession of the Equinoxes, even if their mathematics was unable to predict it numerically."[5]

Mesopotamia

The indigenous religions of the Near East centered in nature and agriculture and, as elsewhere in Neolithic times, focused on images of the Goddess. In Anatolia (now Turkey) around 7000 B.C.E., in the cities of Hacilar and Catal Huyuk, the Goddess was represented in three aspects: young woman, mother giving birth to a child, and crone. Often she was accompanied by a leopard or a bull. The presence of funeral gifts in burials suggests a cult of the dead as well. These Anatolian cultures were followed by the Tell Halaf peoples (again, worshipers of the Goddess), and the Ubaidi (ca. 4300 B.C.E.), who flourished throughout Mesopotamia. The Ubaidi built monumental temples, worked in copper and gold, and developed agriculture and commerce to the highest levels known in prehistoric times.

History begins with writing, and the first people to use writing extensively were the Sumerians of Mesopotamia. No one knows where they came from; their language was not related to any other known tongue, and they seem to have appeared on the scene suddenly and with an already highly developed culture around 4000 B.C.E. Later, beginning perhaps around 3000 B.C.E., groups of Semitic Akkadians began to descend on the Sumerian cities. This resulted first in cultural symbiosis, then in conquest. Around 2300 B.C.E., an Akkadian king, Sargon, established an empire throughout Mesopotamia, which endured for a century before collapsing in the face of attacks by nomads from the upper Tigris. In the centuries that followed, Babylonian and Assyrian empires repeatedly arose from the Akkadian-Sumerian cultural synthesis, exerted temporary supremacy, then fell to barbarians from the north.

That the Babylonians and Assyrians knew of the Solstices is nearly certain (since the excavated temple at Khorsabad in ancient Assyria, modern Iraq, faces northeast, toward the summer Solstice sunrise). But they seem to have placed greater importance on the Equinoxes.

The most important festival in the Babylonian calendar was the beginning of the New Year, which occurred at the spring Equinox (or, in earliest times, at the autumn Equinox). This was the *akitu*, a twelve-day ceremony in which the king, as the son and representative of the divinity, regenerated and synchronized the rhythms of nature, cosmos, and human society.

The main elements of the *akitu* ceremony were as follows:

a. On the first day, the gods of the entire region were invited into the city and the festival. Sacrifices were offered and ritual statuettes fashioned. Then the social order was reversed, so that slaves became masters; all order and hierarchy were abolished, so that the world would symbolically return to chaos.

b. On the fourth day, the priests recited the story of Creation (the *Enuma elish*) in the temples, and two groups of actors mimed the struggle between Marduk (the Creator) and Tiamat (the dragon of chaos).

c. On the fifth day, the chief priest approached the king, stripped him of his royal insignia, and struck him on the cheek. If tears flowed, it was understood that the land would prosper. The king prostrated himself in prayer before restoring his regalia and offering the evening sacrifice.

d. On the eighth day, at a special New Year festival house which was reached by procession and decorated barge, the king and the high priests determined omens for each of the twelve months of the new year in a ceremony called "the fixing of the destinies."

e. Finally, the king (representing Marduk) and a high priestess (representing the divine consort Sarpanitu) entered into hierogamy, or sacred marriage, thus ensuring the fertility of the kingdom. This was followed by a period of collective orgy and feasting that took place beyond the bounds of the city.

The *akitu* ceremony, in its enactment of the yearly return to chaos followed by a new creation, was exemplary of New Year celebrations and festivals throughout the ancient world. As historian of religions Mircea Eliade once put it, "there is everywhere a conception of the end and the beginning of a temporal period, based on the observation of biocosmic rhythms and forming a part of a larger system—the system of periodic purifications (cf. purges, fasting, confession of sins, etc.) and of the periodic regeneration of life."[6]

Canaanites and Hebrews

Between Mesopotamia and Egypt there flourished an agricultural people, referred to in the Bible as Canaanites, whose religion was characterized by the worship of stones and pillars, trees, and sacred wells. Their high god was *El*—a name that appears in the Old Testament in its plural form, *Elohim*. El was at first a generic term for divinity, but later came to refer to the head of the Canaanite pantheon, a sky god called "holy," "merciful," "Father of Gods and Men."

The pantheon included, as principal goddesses, Asherah and Anath; Asherah was the wife of El and the mother of the rest of the gods. The cypress, myrtle, and palm were sacred to her, and her symbol was the two-horned cow. The Canaanites worshiped her through temple prostitution and also through seasonal festivals.

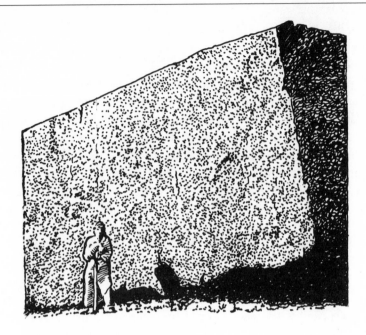

A colossal hewn stone at Baalbek.

While few details of the Canaanite seasonal festivals survive, there is reason to believe that they were synchronized with the Equinoxes and Solstices. The Lebanese town of Baalbek, once known as Heliopolis (the Sun-City), contains the ruins of an ancient temple oriented due east, toward the Equinox sunrise. This temple complex, rebuilt by the Romans, incorporates three hewn stones of extraordinary size that weigh upwards of 750 tons each. Ancient Arab legends say that the first temples of Baal-Astarte at Baalbek were built shortly after the Flood by a tribe of giants.

From the time of Joshua onward, the indigenous Canaanite religion exerted a powerful influence on that of the invading Israelites. Among the latter, the worship of Baal and Astarte, the observance of the local ritual system and sacred sites, the organization of a priestly caste along Canaanite models, and the observance of the seasonal festivals all attested to the depth of this influence. The Israelites, who had been a nomadic, animal-herding people, were becoming agriculturalists, and it must have seemed natural to them to borrow elements from the nature-religion of the farmers among whom they had come to live. Followers of Baal saw the sprouting and decay of vegetation, the ripening of fruits, and the seasonal movement of the Sun as evidence of the activity of their god.

But for the still-nomadic herdsmen of the stony-hilled regions of southern Palestine, the worship of Baal and Astarte seemed to threaten the unique moral and spiritual elements of their own worship of Yahweh. They had come to see human history—rather than nature—as the sphere of divine activity. There was ongoing conflict, therefore, between proponents of Yahwism and Baalism among the Hebrews throughout the first millennium B.C.E.

Nevertheless, the ultimate incorporation of elements of nature-religion into the Judaic heritage is attested by the fact that the most significant ancient religious structure for the Jews (and later for Christians as well), Solomon's fabulous temple at Jerusalem, was oriented to the Equinox sunrise. Each spring Equinox, at the time of the ancient agricultural festival of sowing, sunlight was allowed to penetrate the length of an open passage from the doorway of the temple over the high altar and into the Holy of Holies. It was on this occasion, and this occasion only, that the High Priest entered the *sactum sanctorum*. Norman Lockyer notes that "There is evidence . . . that the entrance of the sunlight on the morning of the spring Equinox formed part of the ceremonial. The priest being in the naos [the Holy Place], the worshipers outside, with their backs to the sun, could see the high priest by means of the sunlight reflected from the jewels in his garment." He quotes a statement of the Roman historian Josephus to the effect that these jewels "shined out when God was present at their sacrifices . . . being seen even by those who were most remote; which splendour yet was not before natural to the stone."[7]

It is of course possible that the observance of the Exquinoxes and Solstices was indigenous to the Hebraic tradition, though I know of no ancient evidence for this. There is, however, a passage in a fifteen-hundred-year-old Jewish commentary in "Abodah Zarah" in the *Babylonian Talmud*, which describes Adam's discovery of the winter Solstice following his expulsion from Eden.

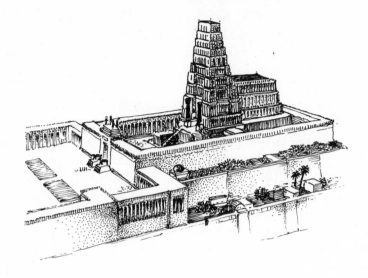

A reconstruction of Solomon's Temple in Jerusalem.

Noticing that the days were growing shorter, he fasted and prayed for eight days; it being exactly Midwinter, his efforts appeared to have succeeded, for soon the days were lengthening again. Every year thereafter, Adam repeated his ritual.

CHAPTER 5

Solstice Rites in the Americas

As WE HAVE JUST SEEN, the ancient inhabitants of Europe and the Near East built spectacular passage chambers, stone circles, temples, and pyramids to mark ceremonially the Solstices and Equinoxes; half a world away, the indigenous peoples of the Americas had no less passionate an interest in the Sun's seasonal cycle. Indeed, for some Native American tribes, the Solstices and Equinoxes served as the temporal cornerstones of culture.

The first people to arrive in the Americas probably came from Asia, perhaps forty thousand years ago (though there is still much controversy about this date among archaeologists). Since Siberian archaeological sites dating to the end of the last Ice Age show signs that the inhabitants kept a lunar calendar,[1] we may assume that early migrants to North America brought with them an already developed concern for times and seasons. This assumption is supported somewhat by the existence of tally marks engraved on rock, found from Oregon to Mexico and as far east as central Nevada, reminiscent of the Paleolithic bone and ivory calendar notations studied by Alexander Marshack. The American petroglyphs appear to be several thousand years old, but unfortunately there is presently no way to date them precisely, since the radiocarbon method works only with organic materials.

However, if we use the basic worldview of surviving Native American peoples as a starting point, we can perform a sort of mythological archaeology that may help us to gain more insight into the thinking of their ancestors several millennia back in time. Two elements common to all North American tribal traditions are a regard for the sacred significance of the four directions of space, and a belief in the existence of a supernatural world—described everywhere in similar celestial imagery—that can be accessed through dreams or visions. Since these ideas are to be found among tribes that are geographically remote and that have dissimilar languages and customs, it seems likely that they were already part of the mythology of the hunters and gatherers who crossed the land bridge from Siberia many millennia ago.

In addition to the two core beliefs mentioned above, many tribes viewed the Solstices and Equinoxes as the temporal equivalents of the four sacred directions and as times when the supernatural world and the mundane world intersect.

The Moundbuilders

About three thousand years ago the people who lived in the valley of the Mississippi and its tributaries began the construction of thousands of earthworks ranging in size from small heaps no bigger than a grave to platforms covering many acres. Some of the more impressive of these mounds were precisely geometrical in shape; others were fashioned in the forms of reptiles, birds, and other animals. While in recent times farmers have destroyed some of these earthworks, and many others that survive await detailed investigation, it is clear that the people who made them commonly oriented these earthen structures astronomically—often to the Solstice and Equinox sunrise points.

The mounds of the Mississippi Valley seem to have been produced throughout a period of over two thousand years by three distinct groups. The first are known as the Adena (we do not

48

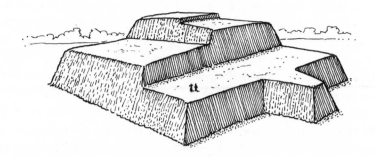

A reconstruction of Cahokia, or Monk's Mound.

know what these people called themselves; as is standard practice in archaeology, they have been given the name of an excavated site), who left behind some of the most intriguing mounds—animal-shaped structures such as the Great Serpent Mound in Adams County, Ohio. After a few centuries, the Adena were gradually supplanted by the Hopewell, who built mounds in the forms of squares, circles, octagons, and straight lines. Last came the Mississippians, who flourished after 1000 C.E. and constructed massive pyramidal platform mounds. The Native Americans of the Mississippi Valley were still using these mounds for ceremonial purposes when Europeans first began colonizing the Americas.

Cahokia, near East St. Louis in southern Illinois, is the most elaborate and best-studied of the Mississippian sites. It was a city of several thousand that flourished between about 800 C.E. and 1550. Built around a ceremonial center of earthen pyramids, Cahokia originally encompassed over a hundred mounds, about eighty of which survive. Monk's Mound, the largest of the complex, is one hundred feet high and sixteen acres in extent. Like others in the complex, it is oriented east-west, toward the equinoctial sunrise.

About a half mile west of Monk's Mound, archaeologists working in the early 1960s found four large circles of post holes. Warren Wittry of the Cranbrook Institute of Science investigated one of these circles in detail and found that it incorporated precise Solstice alignments. Originally, the circle (which Wittry dubbed the "American Woodhenge") consisted of wooden posts two feet wide, set four feet deep; the circle was 410 feet in diameter. Using a backsight post five feet east of the circle's center, the builders sited posts to align with the summer and winter Solstice sunrise points; two other posts align with due east (the equinoctial sunrise) and north. Only about half of the circle is intact, however, so that it was impossible to determine if Solstice sunset points and other astronomical alignments were incorporated into the structure. The size of the circle and the precision of the posthole placement made the Cahokia Woodhenge an accurate calendar, probably used for the determination of seasonal ceremonies and festivals associated with planting.

Circles on the Plains

The nomadic, hunting-and-gathering peoples of the Great Plains had a less complex society than the agricultural Mississippian moundbuilders, whose civilization was apparently influenced by those of Central America; yet the Plains Indians, too, paid close attention to seasons and cycles.

A few tribes, such as the Skidi Pawnee, though they maintained elaborate traditions concerning the stars and timed their ceremonies according to the seasonal motions of the constellations, seem to have had little interest in the Solstices. Nevertheless, most of the tribes from Texas to Canada, from the Mississippi to the Rockies—and particularly the Sioux Nation—participated in a common ceremonial, the Sun Dance, which was traditionally held at the time of the full Moon closest to the summer Solstice. On these yearly occasions, the people camped in a circle around a central cottonwood tree—the Sun Pole. They also built a circular Sun Dance Lodge of twenty-eight poles, with a pole at the center representing *Wakan-Tanka*, the Center of everything. Its entrance was to the east, toward the Equinox sunrise. The entire ceremony was sixteen days in length—eight days of preparation, four days of performance, and four days of abstinence. It was a time of renewal, healing, purification, and prayer. The people's purpose in enacting the Sun Dance was to renew themselves and their world. The timing of the rite—near Midsummer,

The Sun Dance lodge. (After J. E. Brown)

when the Sun is highest in the sky and the days are longest—was all-important.

Thomas Mails, a Lutheran pastor who has written extensively about Native American spiritual traditions, describes the climax of the ceremony:

> When the Sun Dance is done properly, on the last day—and sometimes on one or more of the other days—each of the men called "pledgers" is pierced by having two wooden skewers (or sometimes eagle claws) inserted under the skin of their chests. These skewers are then attached to a strong rope and the other end tied to the Sun Pole. Then the men form a circle around the Sun Pole and, after going forward four times to lay their hands on it and pray, pull back as hard as they are able until the skewers are at last torn free. An alternative method is to have two of the skewers inserted under the skin of the back at shoulder blade height. Heavy buffalo skulls are hung by thongs from these and then dragged around by the bearer until their weight tears the skewers loose.[2]

It is difficult for modern civilized people to understand the ceremonial significance of pain and self-sacrifice within the context of the Native cultures. European-Americans tend to deny or avoid suffering and death at all costs; for the Indians, however, these were essential elements of the wheel of life. There can be no life without sacrifice, pain, and death—whether it be the death of food animals and plants so that the people may live, or of human beings so that future generations and the cosmos itself may live. The Sun Dance provided a focused opportunity for thanksgiving and renewal, and the flesh sacrifice it entailed ensured that it would never be taken lightly.

The Witchita Indians of Kansas built their villages around so-called council circles, which consisted of a central mound surrounded by an elliptical ditch. Archaeologist Waldo Wedel of the Smithsonian Institution investigated three of these circles in Rice County in 1967. He found that they had been built within sight of one another, about a mile apart, and that the lines of sight joining them were aligned with the summer Solstice sunrise and the winter Solstice sunset. He noted also that one of the circles, the Hayes, had its major axis directed toward summer Solstice sunrise; the axis of another, the Tobias circle, was directed toward the summer Solstice sunset.

Further to the west, along the eastern slope of the Rocky Mountains and ranging from Colorado north into Canada, lie the remains of about fifty stone circles known as medicine wheels. Each is composed of small rocks and is centered on a large cairn, or rock pile. Most of the wheels are spoked, and in many cases the spokes are astronomically oriented. The best-studied of these circles are the Bighorn Medicine Wheel on Medicine Mountain near Sheridan, Wyoming, which embodies summer Solstice sunrise and sunset, as well as two stellar alignments; the Fort Smith Medicine Wheel on the Crow Indian Reservation in southern Montana, whose longest spoke points toward Midsummer sunrise; and the Moose Mountain Medicine Wheel in Saskatchewan, which marks the same celestial events as the Bighorn wheel. The Bighorn Medicine Wheel has twenty-eight spokes, the number of poles in the traditional Sun Dance lodge.

The medicine wheels are difficult to date, and it has so far proven difficult to determine who built them or how they were used. It seems likely, however, that they were involved in seasonal

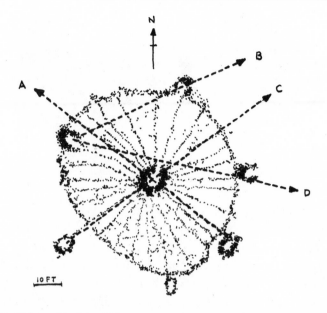

The Bighorn Medicine Wheel in Wyoming. The alignments indicated are: A. Summer Solstice sunset; B. Aldebaran rises; C. Summer Solstice sunrise; and D. Rigel rises.

rites similar to the Sun Dance—at which people from hundreds of miles around gathered for several days of celebration, ceremony, and prayers to the Above Beings.

Solstice Lightshows in Ancient California

The Chumash Indians of the central Pacific coast of California saw the Solstices as times when the Earth, human society, and the Cosmos all reached points of crisis. On these occasions, the survival of the world depended upon the people's performance of appropriate ceremonies.

Perhaps because their food source was abundant, the Chumash occupied permanent settlements (unlike most other hunter-gatherers) and developed a complex and stratified society. At the time of first contact with Europeans, in 1542, they were organized into two provinces, one ruled by a woman. At the top of the

Sun symbols from various Chumash rock paintings.

Chumash social pyramid were a religious elite, the *'antap*, among whom were astronomer-shamans whose duty it was to maintain the calendar and to determine the appropriate times for ceremonies.

Chumash mythology centered on the motions of celestial bodies. These were thought to have formerly been humans, who had ascended from the Earth long ago to escape from a world catastrophe—the primeval flood described in so many cultures' traditions. The most important and powerful of the sky beings was the Sun, who lived in a quartz crystal house. The Sun was believed to lead a team of sky people in an ongoing daily ball game in which the opposing team was led by Sky Coyote (the North Star), whom the people viewed as their benefactor. Moon kept score. The game was concluded each year at winter Solstice, when there was a real danger that the Sun's team might win and decide not to return, thus upsetting the balance of nature.

For the Chumash, the Solstices were revelations of the cosmic order. The people themselves ritually participated in that order by helping to restore the Moon to life each month through their prayers and shouts, and by averting cosmic catastrophe each Midwinter. The astronomer-shaman, the *'alchuklash*, played a key role in the latter drama by maintaining a vigil in a special Sun-watching cave, and alerting his people of the arrival of the Solstice. When the time came, several days of ceremonies ensued, presided over by the high chief, the *paha*, who was considered the "Image of the Sun." Also during this time shamans consumed the sacred psychedelic herb *datura*, and the people participated in dances symbolizing the soul's journey along the Milky Way to the land of the dead.

The Chumash produced some of the finest rock art in North America, much of which centered on the mythic significance of the Solstice. At many cave sites in the region between modern Los Angeles and Santa Barbara, spotlighting effects have been observed on Midwinter morning. For example, at Burro Flats, just beyond the northeast corner of San Fernando Valley, a complex collection of animal and geometric images is shaded throughout the year by a canopy of rock; then, on the morning of the winter Solstice, a triangle of sunlight cuts to the center of a series of concentric rings before shrinking back to the base of the prepared rock surface. Similar effects have been observed at Condor Cave in the Los Padres National Forest, at Window Cave at Vandenberg Air Force Base, and at La Rumorosa in Baja, where a dagger of sunlight illuminates a white circle, then cuts precisely across the eyes of a thirteen-inch high shaman figure, as if to symbolize his magical participation in the event.

Other West Coast tribes, from present-day Baja to British Columbia, shared a similar concern for the Solstices. For example, further north in California—in Sonoma and Mendocino counties—the Pomo Indians called the Solstices the times of "starting back." Each valley was watched by a special Sun priest who noted the position of sunrise each day in relation to a particular hill on the horizon, and thereby kept track of the Sun's progress toward a Solstice. When sunrise occurred in the same spot for four consecutive days, the sunwatcher proclaimed the Solstice.

Sun Priests of the Southwest

Late in the morning of June 29, 1977, Anna Sofaer, an artist with an interest in prehistoric Indian petroglyphs, made a treacherous 430-foot climb to the top of Fajada Butte in Chaco Canyon in New Mexico to photograph two spirals carved high on the butte's eastern face. The carvings were shaded by three large, parallel slabs of rock. But as Sofaer knelt to capture the carvings on film, she noticed a thin dagger of sunlight moving vertically down the larger

The figure of a shaman, painted in red, on the wall of La Rumorosa, a rock shelter in Baja California. On the winter Solstice, a triangle of light crosses the shaman's face.

spiral, just to the right of its center. The timing of her arrival at the site turned out to have been all-important: it was noon and, as she then realized, only a few days past Midsummer. As she later told an audience at the Los Alamos Laboratory, "it occurred to me that the spiral was put there to record [the Solstice]. A week earlier the light would have passed through the center. It was an incredible coincidence that I was there just a few days past the summer Solstice, at noon. If I had come a little later or earlier [in the day], I would have missed the whole thing."[3]

The next year, Sofaer returned to Fajada Butte, accompanied by physicist Rolf M. Sinclair and Volker Zinser, an architect familiar with spotlighting effects. Beginning in mid-May, they recorded the play of sunlight across the two spirals and studied the rock surfaces that shaped the sliver of light. On June 21, the sunbeam

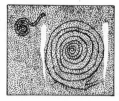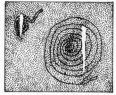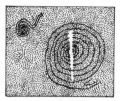

The light and shadow effect on the petroglyphs at Fajada Butte in Chaco Canyon. Left: winter Solstice; center: the Equinoxes; right: summer Solstice.

moved precisely through the center of the larger spiral. But they noticed a much smaller, second spot of sunlight to the left. Could it have a function as well, they wondered? They returned at the fall Equinox, and found that now one of the light beams bisected the smaller spiral (the same effect occurs at the spring Equinox); and when they returned yet again at the winter Solstice, they observed the two streaks of light framing the larger spiral. Here, in a single stone structure, ancient astronomers had found a way to mark each of the Solstices and Equinoxes with a unique spot-lighting effect.

Sofaer and Zinser became convinced, for a variety of reasons, that the rock slabs were deliberately positioned and carefully shaped in order to produce the lighting effects. A later geological survey cast doubt on the idea that the native astronomers had in fact moved the slabs into place; even so, they had clearly taken masterful advantage of the situation. "The monumental quality of this solar construct," wrote Kendrick Frazier in *Science News*, ". . . is characterized by the Indians' sensitive integration of their structures with nature, light, and patterns of the solar cycle."[4]

Chaco Canyon is the largest of hundreds of ruins throughout the American Southwest that are attributed to the *Anasazi*, a Navajo word for "the ancient ones," who, according to some experts, were the ancestors of the modern Hopi and Zuni Indians. Their complex and widespread culture flourished between 400 and 1300 C.E., when it apparently succumbed—as have so many civilizations—to the exhaustion of local environmental resources.

The Anasazi built a remarkable series of roads and ceremonial centers, but apparently did not have an oppressive social hierarchy or wealthy ruling class. While the Anasazi had no system of writing by which to record their spiritual beliefs, their ruins offer direct evidence of these people's profound interest in the Sun's seasonal journey.

Casa Rinconada, a *kiva* (or underground circular ceremonial chamber), and Casa Bonita, an Anasazi town that once housed perhaps six thousand people, are located not far from Fajada Butte in Chaco Canyon National Monument. Casa Rinconada has a wall niche that is illuminated by the Sun at summer Solstice sunrise, and the corner windows of Pueblo Bonito permitted observation of the winter Solstice sunrise. At another site, in Hovenweep National Monument in the Four Corners region, archaeoastronomer Dr. Ray Williamson has studied a solar shrine that, like the one at Fajada, was used to track both the Solstices and the Equinoxes. It consists of two small, angled windows in an otherwise gloomy room on the ground floor of a fortress-like ruin. The windows are so placed that at Midwinter sunset the Sun appears through one window and casts a beam on the far wall; at Midsummer it appears through the other window; and at the Equinoxes two sunbeams can be seen, each lined up with one of the low doorways by which the room is accessed.

Since the Anasazi left no writings, we can only speculate about the nature of their Solstice celebrations. But the Anasazi's present-day descendants, the Zuni and Hopi Indians, have astronomically-based rites that may, in their general outlines at least, date back many centuries to the time when Chaco Canyon was a thriving cultural center.

For the Zuni, the winter Solstice is the time of the *Shalako*, an elaborate night-long ceremony—still performed today and observed by thousands of tourists—that includes appearances by the *Katchina* priest and clowns and the *Shalako* themselves—twelve-foot-high bird-headed effigies regarded as messengers from the gods. The timing of the rite is all-important, and in former days it was entrusted to the *Pekwin*, or Sun Priest. It was his task to ensure that the *Shalako* ceremony coincided as closely as possible with both *itiwanna*, the exact day of the winter Solstice, and also the full Moon.

The *Pekwin* observed the Sun at dawn and sunset by watching its place of appearance or disappearance on the horizon from fixed viewing points—a petrified stump at the edge of the village, a "Sun tower," or a small, semicircular stone shrine. Before both the summer and winter Solstice, the Sun Priest traditionally undertook eight days of ritual prayer and fasting, during which he made pilgrimages to the sacred Thunder Mountain and communed with the Sun Father. On the ninth morning, he announced the approach of the Solstice with a call that was, as ethnologist Frank Cushing described it in the 1880s, "low, mournful, yet strangely penetrating and tuneful."

But the *Pekwin* had no monopoly on the observation of the solar cycle. Cushing noted that

. . . many are the houses in Zuni with scores on their walls or ancient plates imbedded therein, while opposite a con-venient window or small port-hole lets in the light of the rising sun, which shines but two mornings in three hundred and sixty-five on the same place. Wonderfully reliable and ingenious are these rude systems of orientation by which the religion, the labors and even the pastimes of the Zunis are regulated.[5]

The Hopi Sun Chief had duties similar to those of the Zuni *Pekwin*. During the winter, he would sit on the roof of the Sun Clan house in the village of Walpi and from there watch the Sun set over the distant San Francisco mountains. When it reached a dip beside the southernmost peak, he proclaimed the time for the night-long Solstice ceremony of the kindling of fire.

The Hopi sunwatcher was not only concerned with the Sol-stices, however. The planting of crops, as well as the timing of the year-long cycle of Hopi ceremonies, was tied to the position of the Sun. In his 1931 paper on "The Hopi Ceremonial Calendar" in the *Museum Notes* of the Museum of Northern Arizona, Edmund N. Nequatewa wrote:

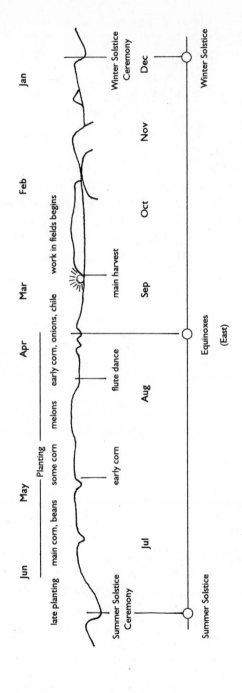

The Hopi horizon calendar.

The cycle of Hopi ceremonies begins in the winter. The dates of all the winter ceremonies are established by watching the position of the sun as it sets on the western horizon, while those of the summer ceremonies are fixed by the position of the rising sun on the eastern horizon. . . .

The first of the winter ceremonies is in November. When the sun sets over a particular hump on the north side of the San Francisco Peaks, the ceremony, Wu-Wu-che-ma, takes place. Four societies take part. . . .

After this ceremony is over, they again watch the sun on the western horizon. They just know on a certain day that it will take the sun eight days to reach its southernmost point, and they announce the ceremony for eight days ahead. Thus, Sol-ya-lang-eu, the Prayer-Offering Ceremony, is the Winter Solstice Ceremony, and takes place in December. This is one of the most sacred ceremonies of the Hopi. It is a day of good will, when every man wishes for prosperity and health, for his family and friends. . . .[6]

Just after the summer Solstice, the Hopi celebrate a festival they call *Niman Kachina*. It is the time when the *kachinas*—the spirits of the invisible forces of life—return home to the the spiritworld. When it is the summer Solstice in this Earth, it is winter Solstice in the lower world, and in this way balance is maintained in the universe. The Niman Kachina celebration is focused on a ceremony of the four energies—the germination of plants, the heat of the Sun, the life-giving qualities of water, and the magnetic forces in the Earth and atmosphere. The Hopi use spruce branches in the ceremony because these are believed to have a magnetic force that draws rain.

In their precise observations of the Sun's stations, the Hopi, the Zuni, and presumably the Anasazi were not motivated by the desire for scientific knowledge. Their calendars were not attempts to objectify time in the familiar (to us) categories of past, present, and future, but were rather mythological and ritual constructs. These peoples were driven by an overwhelming concern for being "in tune" with cosmic cycles. The Hopi see everything in nature in terms of complementary principles—life and death, summer and winter, day and night. It is their duty, they believe, to maintain the balance of the forces of nature and cosmos through ritual activity. The Solstices and Equinoxes are special opportunities for human beings to celebrate and reinforce that balance.

Astronomical Temples of Mexico

An hour's drive northeast of Mexico City lie the restored ruins of Teotihuacan, the largest city of pre-Columbian America and a source of continuing mystery for archaeologists. We still do not know who built the city, what language the builders spoke, or where they went after it was destroyed.

At its height, Teotihuacan's population reached 170,000 or more—comparable with that of Imperial Rome. The city's construction was begun around 200 B.C.E., according to most archaeologists (though a few suggest much earlier dates), and around 100 C.E. work commenced on two enormous pyramids. The larger of these, the Pyramid of the Sun, covers about the same land area as the Great Pyramid of Gizeh, though it rises to about half the latter structure's height, or just over two hundred feet. In the years after 250 C.E., Teotihuacan's influence spread throughout Mesoamerica, and other cities were modelled after it. Around 750, however, it was destroyed by fire and abandoned, perhaps as the result of invasion or a natural catastrophe.

Teotihuacan was laid out according to a strict right-angle grid pattern. This prodigious feat of surveying was accomplished with the help of numerous cross-and-circle markers chipped into rock surfaces and temple floors throughout the surrounding region. But the axis of the city's streets, temples, public baths, ball courts, theaters, and apartment houses is about sixteen degrees askew of the cardinal directions. Why this peculiar orientation?

The answer seems to lie in an alignment at right angles to the main avenue of the city. In the first and second centuries of the common era, the Pleiades set just before dawn at the western horizon point marked by the alignment on the morning of the

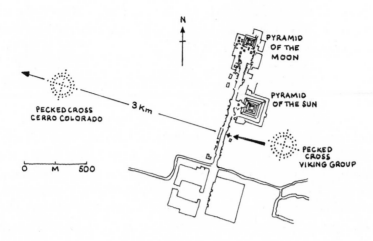

The Street of the Dead in Teotihuacan is precisely perpendicular
to a line joining two pecked crosses. That line points to the place
on the horizon where the Sun rises on the summer Solstice.

one day of the year when (at this latitude) the Sun shines directly
overhead, casting no shadows. This "zenith day" occurs on the
Equinoxes at the equator, and at the summer Solstice at the tropic
of Cancer and the Tropic of Capricorn. Between the equator and
the tropic lines, the date varies according to latitude; north or
south of the tropics, there is no zenith day. The phenomenon of
the shadowless noon is a striking one, and virtually all Central
American cultures accorded it great significance. But at Teotihuacan, this solar event was compounded with a stellar one: on the
night before the shadowless day, the Pleiades passed through the
zenith at about midnight, when the Sun was at anti-zenith. Then,
as the Pleiades set in the west, the Sun rose in the east; and when
the Sun reached zenith at noon, the Pleiades were in turn directly
underfoot at anti-zenith, metaphorically in the underworld. The
Sun and the Pleiades may therefore have served to represent to
the Teotihuacans the universal complementary principles of light
and dark, life and death, this world and the next.

There is evidence that the builders of Teotihuacan were so
concerned with the zenith day that they sought to establish the

location of the Tropic of Cancer. Less than three miles north of the line of the Tropic, Charles Kelley of the University of Southern Illinois found more cross-and-circle symbols almost identical to the ones at Teotihuacan; their axes point to the place on the horizon where the Sun rises at Midsummer, the day it also passes through the zenith at noon at the Tropic.

The Pyramid of the Sun, meanwhile, served as an Equinox indicator. The lower part of the pyramid's fourth level is boldly outlined and visible for miles; it is so angled that during the morning on the Equinoxes it is in shadow, but just at noon local time the Sun's rays reach it. Then, two days after the Equinox, the shadow on the north face "flashes" on and off at midday. The knowledge and skill required of the architects in order to produce these effects must have been considerable.

In his 1976 book *Mysteries of the Mexican Pyramids*, Peter Tompkins traced the history of the exploration of Teotihuacan and summarized over two centuries of speculations about its builders' identity, purposes, and abilities, presenting at some length the views of Hugh Harleston, Jr., an American engineer who became fascinated with the ruined city and spent years analyzing its astronomical and geodetic functions. Harleston theorized both that Teotihuacan was built around units of measure identical with those used in the ancient Near East (as in the Great Pyramid), and that the designers incorporated into their ceremonial structures significant numbers relating to the dimensions of the Earth, the orbital distances of the planets, etc. In Harleston's view, the city was meant to serve (among other things) as an accurate map of the heavens. Harleston located numerous sight-lines joining temples and pyramids throughout the city, by which the summer and winter Solstices and the Equinoxes might have been marked.

The people of Teotihuacan, like those of other Central American civilizations, no doubt saw the lights in the sky as representing a cosmic hierarchy of divine beings; the kings and nobles of the terrestrial world were their appointed representatives, and human events like wars and natural disasters were seen as reflections of confrontations between and among the cosmic powers. By organizing their city according to a celestial design, and by enacting ceremonies at cosmically significant times (such as the Solstices and Equinoxes), the people of Teotihuacan sought to establish and maintain precarious balances between order and chaos, freedom and security—balances that every civilization strives for, but that few are able to keep for long.

Mayan and Aztec Skywatchers

To the south of Teotihuacan lived the Mayas, whose high culture flourished in the present-day Mexican states of Chiapas, Tabasco, Yucatan, and Campeche, the Mexican territory of Quintana Roo, as well as in Guatemala and Belize and parts of Honduras and El Salvador. We know that Mayan civilization ended about 900 C.E., when it gradually succumbed, perhaps to political disintegration and the invasions of nomadic tribes. Its beginnings are less certain, however, and keep getting pushed back in time by archaeologists (the current estimate is something like 2500 B.C.E.). Like the people of Teotihuacan, the Mayas were prodigious builders and sophisticated astronomers. Indeed, their knowledge of the sky was as detailed and accurate as that of any ancient people whose works have survived and been deciphered.

The Toltecs, who conquered the Mayan city of Chichén Itzá and presided over a cultural renaissance there until shortly after 1200, had an annual solar calendar fixed at 365 days with a leap year every fourth year. The Classic Maya, in contrast, used the day as their fundamental unit of time. Their sophisticated arithmetic, by which they computed dates in the millions of days, incorporated place-value notation and the concept of zero. Using the day-unit, the Maya synchronized lunar months, solar years, planetary phases, eclipses, and other celestial phenomena, and correlated them with the events of their own political history. They thereby became the first people in the world to integrate celestial and terrestrial time in a single, comprehensive system.

Like the Babylonians, the Maya held an attitude toward time, astronomy, and mathematics that was not so much scientific (in the modern sense) as astrological. All their observations were regarded as omens for rulers and their families; their elaborate computations

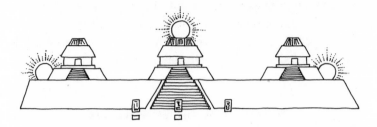

The temple group at Uaxactun, as viewed from the steps of Pyramid of Group E. The Equinox sunrise appears over the center temple; the summer Solstice sunrise appears at the corner of the left temple, and the winter Solstice sunrise at the corner of the right temple. (After Krupp)

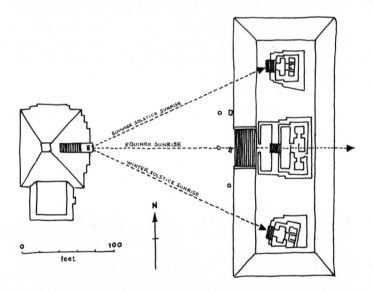

The Solstice and Equinox alignments from the pyramid of Group E at Uaxactun.

represented an obsessive search for a system of numbers that would encompass both the motions of celestial bodies and the events of human history in a unified scheme capable of foretelling the fortunes of a wealthy elite.

Solar alignments have been found at many Mayan sites. One of the most remarkable examples consists of a group of temples at Uaxactun, a ceremonial center in the Guatemalan jungle. If one stands at the top step of the western pyramid and faces east, sunrise occurs over three small, equally-spaced buildings on a great stone platform. The placement of the northern and southern buildings permits accurate determination of the Solstices; on the Equinoxes, the Sun rises immediately above the central temple. This alignment scheme was copied in at least a dozen other Mayan cities.

An even more intriguing set of orientations was incorporated into a tower at Chichén Itzá. Known as the Caracol because of an inner spiral stairway (*caracol* being Spanish for "snail"), the structure seems to have been used as a multipurpose observatory. Nearly all the walls, doors, and windows of the Caracol are asymmetrically situated. But, using them as sighting lines, it is possible to mark the Solstices and Equinoxes, as well as the rising or setting points of several bright stars and the planet Venus.

Our understanding of the Maya's astronomy is greatly facilitated by the fact that theirs was a literate civilization. In addition to their temples and observatories we have a few surviving writings in native Mayan which record that people's mythology and worldview (though most such writings were tragically burned by the Inquisition). Among these is a book from the colonial period that is traditionally attributed to Chilam Balam, a legendary sage and scholar. In a section on Mayan astronomical knowledge and practice it is recorded:

> When the eleventh day of June shall come, it will be the longest day, when the thirteenth of September comes, this day and night are precisely the same length. When the twelfth day of December shall come, the day is short, but the night is long. When the tenth day of March comes, the day and the night will be equal in length.[7]

The translator, Ralph Roys, notes that "This date for the summer Solstice indicates that the passage was originally written at a time when the Julian calendar was still current in the Yucatan."

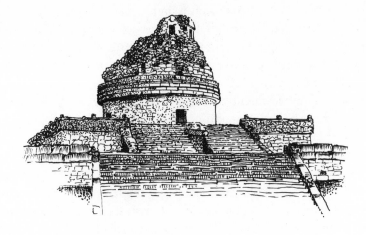

The ruins of the Caracol at Chichén Itzá.

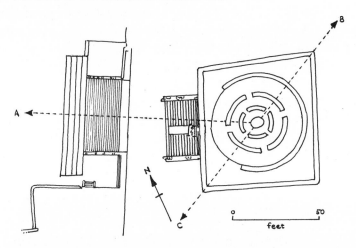

The plan of the Caracol, showing alignments to: A, summer Solstice sunset; B, summer Solstice sunrise; and C, winter Solstice sunset.

Much of the mystery surrounding the ancient Maya is currently being dispelled by the study of their surviving Central American descendants, who have preserved much of their cultural heritage. Among the modern Maya, the priestly or shamanic function is performed by individuals known as "daykeepers" or "sunkeepers." One of the duties of the daykeeper is to regulate the calendar by observing the Solstices and Equinoxes. Near the town of Nebaj, Guatemala, American anthropologist J. Steward Lincoln found that such observations were still being facilitated (as of 1940) by the use of towers, standing stones, and stone circles similar to ones that date back to the earliest Pre-Classic period of Mayan culture.

The Aztecs of southern Mexico presided over the last, brief flourishing of native civilization in Central America. They built what was unquestionably among the most violent societies that has ever existed: their cities fed on incessant human sacrifice (which was, incidentally, not unknown to the Mayas), and their pantheon consisted almost entirely of demons. And yet Aztec songs and poetry dwell endlessly on images of magical birds and flowers. Ptolemy Tompkins suggests in his brilliant and disturbing book *This Tree Grows out of Hell: Mesoamerica and the Search for the Magical Body* that the Mayan/Aztec obsession with death may have been the end result of a gradual corruption of the tribal shaman's ecstatic flight from the body, and of the universal longing to return to an original, ideal paradise by shedding the mortal coil. With civilization, it seems, comes alienation not only from the Earth but also from the wellsprings of renewal within the human body and psyche; human sacrifice served as these people's desperate attempt to reach the steadily-receding Otherworld:

> Whereas the Maya appear to have practiced human sacrifice primarily as a method of personal, individual aggrandizement, sacrifice among the Aztecs was a far greater entity. . . . Sacrifice was a primary cosmic principle in this universe—an a priori factor as important as time and space, and hence an essential tool for human beings desiring to enter into contact with the supernatural forces that gave shape to the world.[8]

At the time of Montezuma—the last ruler of the intact Aztec empire, who died at the hands of Cortez—sacrificial victims routinely waited in lines up to a mile long to have their hearts ritually torn from their chests and held up to the four directions. Even battle-hardened Spanish soldiers were revolted by the stench of death that clung to the bloodstained stairways of the Aztec pyramids.

If indeed the Aztecs' methodical rites of human sacrifice were the decadent expression of a longing for the experience of shamanic ecstasy, they occurred in a context that preserved other elements of the shamanic worldview in corrupted form as well. As we have seen, many ancient peoples kept track of the Solstices by means of simple sighting sticks or standing stones. The Aztecs likewise celebrated the Sun's seasonal motions, but used a far more elaborate means to do so.

The ceremonial focus of Tenochtitlan, the Aztec capital, was the Templo Mayor, a pyramid surmounted by two symmetrical temples. Immediately to the west, across a plaza, stood a smaller, cylindrical Temple of Quetzalcoatl. According to archaeoastronomer Anthony Aveni, who surveyed the site, the Templo Mayor was "a functioning astronomical observatory" whose main purpose was to announce the Equinoxes. One morning each spring and autumn, observers standing on the steps of the Temple of Quetzalcoatl would see the Sun rise in the notch between the two temples atop the eastern pyramid.

The fact that the Aztecs aligned their principal religious structure with the equinoctial sunrise is partly to be explained by the fact that they celebrated the main festival of the god Xipe Totec at the vernal Equinox. But it may have another, darker significance as well. An illustration of the legend of the founding of Tenochtitlan in 1325 in the Aztec *Codex Mendoza* shows an eagle using its talons to rip the fruit from a cactus. The eagle symbolized the Sun, and the cactus fruit was the equivalent of a human heart. In the minds of the Aztecs, the main purpose for their painstakingly choreographed rituals of human sacrifice was *to keep the Sun alive*. Perhaps they perceived the Equinoxes as signs of reassurance that their efforts were effectual.

Solar Rites in South America

The Andean Incas began their ascent to empire about three hundred years before the voyage of Columbus, building on foundations laid by a long series of native Peruvian cultures. When Francisco Pizarro arrived in the early sixteenth century, he found a highly organized socialist society stretching fifteen hundred miles from Equador to Chile, with a population of perhaps six million. The Incan economic system lacked markets, merchants, or money, yet managed to provide a sufficiency of food and other basic necessities for all. Other achievements included monumental stone fortresses, suspension bridges, an extraordinary legacy of cultivated medicinal and food plants (including many varieties of potato and maize), and a system of paved roads and runners by which messages could be sent a distance of 150 miles in a day.

The Incan high god was the nameless Source of all life, whom they addressed by the title *Wiraqoca* (or *Viracocha*). Popular religious rites were devoted to lesser deities, such as *Pachamama*, the Earth mother; *Inti*, the Sun; as well as the gods and goddesses of the Moon, sea, and thunder; and to the *huacas*, a collection of over three hundred sacred sites that included springs, fountains, caves, hills, tombs, and houses. At the center of the Incas' capital, Cuzco, stood the *Coricancha* (or Sun Temple), oriented toward the winter Solstice sunrise, in whose innermost shrine were hung magnificent solid gold Sun discs.

According to the Inca creation myth, the first Incas (the young emperor and his sister-bride) were sent to Earth from their father, the Sun, to find the place where a golden rod he had given them could be plunged into the soil. This mythic rod probably represents the Sun's perfectly vertical rays at noon on zenith day.

Around 1600, Garcilaso de la Vega, the son of a Spanish captain and nephew of the eleventh Inca ruler, compiled his *Royal Commentaries of the Incas*, in which he described a sacred group of gnomons, or Sun-sticks, near Quito, which lies close to the equator. There, the Equinox Sun passes through the zenith at noon, affording the *Inti*, in Garcilaso's words, "the seat he liked best, since there he sat straight up and elsewhere on one side." North or south of the equator, the zenith days and the Equinoxes are not synchronized; but Incas at all latitudes throughout the tropics watched their gnomons until "at midday the sun bathed all sides of the column and cast no shadows at all. . . . Then they decked the columns with all the flowers and aromatic herbs they could find and placed the throne of the sun on it, saying that on that day the sun was seated on the column in all his full light."[9]

From the Sun Temple in Cuzco, forty-one imaginary lines or *ceque* radiated out, each marked along its length by *huacas*. Anthony Aveni has demonstrated that one of the more prominent *ceque* served as a sighting line to a hilltop *huaca*, which was the foresight for the viewing of the December (summer) Solstice sunset from the Coricancha temple. The functions of other *ceque*, as well as those of the famous and mysterious lines on the Nazca plain, remain unknown.

Two of the Incas' most important festivals were held on the Solstices. *Inti Raymi* was the winter Solstice festival, held in June; the summer ceremony, *Capac Raymi*, was held in December. Astronomer E. C. Krupp describes the *Inti Raymi* rite as follows:

> Before dawn on the day of the winter Solstice the Sapa Inca [the emperor] and the curacas in the royal lineage went to the Haucaypata, a ceremonial plaza in central Cuzco. There, they took off their shoes as a sign of deference to the sun, faced the northeast, and waited for the sunrise. As soon as the sun appeared, everyone crouched, much as we would get down on our knees, and blew respectful kisses to the glowing gold disk. The Sapa Inca then lifted two golden cups of *chicha*, the sacred beer of fermented corn, and offered the one in his left hand to the sun. It was then poured into a basin and disappeared into channels that conducted it away as though the sun had consumed it. After sipping the blessed chicha in the other cup, the Sapa Inca shared it with the others present with him and then walked to the Coricancha. . . .[10]

For the *Sapa Inca*, the day's ceremonies continued in the Coricancha's Sun Room, which was lined with gold plates. A fire was lit by focusing the Sun's rays with a concave mirror, and sacrifices followed.

During the past few decades, the Kogi Indians have watched as the climate has changed in the Andes mountains of Colombia as the result of pollution and deforestation. They regard the civilized white race as the "younger brother," and have issued a warning that unless the younger brother desists in ravaging the natural environment, the Earth herself will sicken and die. In 1990, the Kogi were the subject of a ninety-minute BBC television documentary produced by Alan Eleira, titled "From the Heart of the World: the Elder Brother's Warning." Eleira has more recently produced a book on the Kogi, *Elder Brothers*.

The Kogi visualize the cosmos as a great spindle with nine levels, and oriented in six directions (up, down, northwest, southeast, southwest, and northwest). The latter four directions refer to the sunrise and sunset extremes at the Solstices. Kogi temples are patterned after the spindle-shaped universe. The Kogi *mama*, or shaman, lays out the groundplan of the temple with a cord and stake. He locates the four corners of the structure by lining the cord up with the summer and winter Solstice sunrise and sunset points on the horizon. At noon on the June Solstice, the Sun shines through a hole in the very top of the temple—which the *mama* uncovers for the occasion—and from dawn to sunset moves between carefully positioned fireplaces. The Kogi liken the movement of the Sun to the act of weaving. E. C. Krupp writes: "Through the year, as the sun moves north, south, and north again, it is said to spiral about the world spindle. It weaves the thread of life into an orderly fabric of existence, and the cyclical changes of the sun's daily path are transformed into a cloth of light on the temple floor."[11] The Kogi believe that it is the duty of human beings to assist in the weaving process, and to order their own lives according to the warp and weft of the universal pattern.

In the Amazon, the Equinoxes coincide with the start of the two rainy seasons—one in March, the other in September. The Desana and Barasana Indians see connections between everything that happens on Earth—and particularly, the availability of fish and game animals—with what they see in the sky. They see the night sky as a great brain, with its two hemispheres divided by the

Milky Way. According to the Desana-Barasana creation myths, on the First Day the Sun Father fertilized the world at its center by there erecting a perfectly vertical rod. It was from this spot that the first people emerged. The place where the Desana-Barasana believe this primordial event occurred happens to lie almost exactly on the equator. Thus, each spring and fall Equinox, when the Sun is directly overhead, and an upright staff casts no shadow, the Desana and Barasana believe the Sun's rays are again directly penetrating the Earth, making the world fertile and new.

CHAPTER **6**

Festivals of Heaven and Earth in the Far East, India, and Polynesia

CHINA IS NEARLY UNIQUE among the world's cultures in that its mythology contains no memory of ancient folk migrations. The Chinese believed that they originated where they are today, and they called their land the Middle Kingdom—the center of the world. Moreover the earliest Chinese mythology, rather than describing the creation of the Universe and the origin of evil, tells instead of the first Emperors, who are said to have developed agriculture, the domestication of animals, and writing. This legendary history extends back to about 3000 B.C.E. While most Western historians regard the legendary first Emperors as purely fictional, the Chinese people continue to believe in them and are somewhat justified in doing so by the fact that theirs is unquestionably one of the oldest continuous civilizations on Earth.

Yao, the fourth of these legendary Emperors, is said to have devised a calendar for the purpose of regulating agricultural activity throughout the land. The Book of Records describes instructions which "the Perfect Emperor Yao [in 2254 B.C.E. gave] to his astronomers to ascertain the solstices and equinoxes. . . and fix the four seasons. . . ."

From its beginning, Chinese astronomy served an oracular function. Priests of the Shang dynasty (1500-1100 B.C.E.) recorded celestial observations on engraved bones, which they then exposed to fire so as to "read" the answers to their questions in cracks formed by the heat. Later, when the country was unified under the Emperors, astronomy became the province of a government department, and consisted of carefully recording celestial phenomena (particularly the unusual ones, such as eclipses and comets) and then interpreting their astrological significance not only for the state, but for nearly every aspect of the daily life of the people.

To the modern scientific astronomer, the traditional Chinese stargazers present a paradox. On one hand, their accuracy and persistence resulted in the production of the most complete and reliable record in existence of eclipses, comets, and supernovae for the past two millennia. On the other hand, however, their preoccupation with bureaucracy and mythology kept the Chinese from making even the most rudimentary inquiries into the mechanics of solar, lunar, and planetary motions.

At the time of the Shang dynasty, according to indications on a few of the thousands of oracle bones that have been recovered and studied, the year was divided into quarters (bounded by the Equinoxes and Solstices) by measuring the length of the shadow cast by a gnomon, or Sun-stick. The Shou dynasty, which followed the Shang in 1100 B.C.E., left behind hundreds of pyramids in the Wei River valley of the Shensi province, many of which appear to incorporate celestial alignments. A significant number are oriented to the Equinox sunrise. Unfortunately, however, we know little about the exact nature of the seasonal rites of the preimperial era because virtually all books and records were destroyed in 213 B.C.E. by the edict of the first Emperor, Qin Shihuangdi. At around that time, however, the imperial court instituted calendrical rites that continued with little alteration until the early twentieth century. The beginning of the year was situated halfway between the winter Solstice and the vernal Equinox, in the middle of February. But significant festivals were held on the summer and winter Solstices, when the Emperor symbolically renewed the world order.

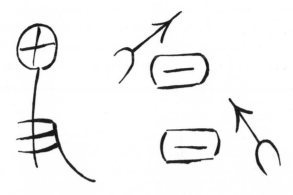

Shang characters carved in oracle bones. The character at left may represent a gnomon used to determine the solstices. The ones at right may portray the sun, with shadows of human figures shown at differing angles to indicate different times of the year.

Three days before the Midwinter ceremony, the Emperor began a process of purification, abstaining from women, music, certain foods, and other activities. Then, two hours before sunrise on the morning of the Solstice, a procession of royalty, officials, musicians, singers, and dancers brought him to the Round Mound in Beijing's Temple of Heaven just south of the Forbidden City.

Norman Lockyer quotes an account of the ceremony that followed, written by an explorer named Edkins in the nineteenth century, when these yearly Solstice ceremonies were still being performed:

> The Emperor, with his immediate suite, kneels in front of the tablet of Shang-Ti and faces north. The platform is laid with marble stones, forming nine concentric circles; the inner circle consists of nine stones, cut so as to fit with close edges round the central stone, which is a perfect circle. Here the Emperor kneels, and is surrounded first by the circles of the terraces and their enclosing walls, and then by the circle of the horizon. He thus seems to himself and his court to be in the centre of the universe,

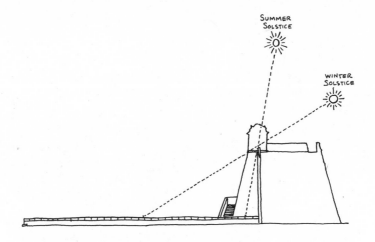

The observatory of Guan Xing Tai at Gao Cheng Zhen, constructed in 1279 C.E. The differences in the lengths of the shadows cast at the summer and winter Solstices by the horizontal rod at the opening of the forty-foot tower enabled precise measurement of the tropical year. (After Krupp)

and turning to the north, assuming the attitude of a subject, he acknowledges in prayer and by his position that he is inferior to heaven, and to heaven alone. Round him on the pavement are the nine circles of as many heavens, consisting of nine stones, then eighteen, then twenty-seven, and so on in successive multiples of nine till the square of nine, the favourite number of Chinese philosophy, is reached in the outermost circle of eighty-one stones.

The same symbolism is carried throughout the balustrades, the steps, and the two lower terraces of the altar. Four flights of steps of nine each lead down to the middle terrace, where are placed the tablets to the spirits of the sun, moon, and stars and the year god, Tai-sui.[1]

After lighting a fire, the Emperor read an account of the last year and made ceremonial sacrifices to heaven, consisting of

78

The view south along the shadow measuring wall to the tower. The horizontal bar (reconstructed) casts a shadow on the wall, permitting the exact calculation of the Solstices. (After Krupp)

incense, jade, and silk. Finally, a portion of roasted human flesh from a sacrificial victim was offered up. After bowing nine times to the north, the Emperor descended the Round Mound.

The summer Solstice ceremony was a complement to the December rite. While the winter festival was held to honor and energize the celestial, male, *yang* forces in order to counterbalance the natural predominance of *yin* that occurs in that season, the summer celebration was earthy, feminine, and *yin* in character so as to stimulate those forces when they are naturally at their weakest. The summer rite took place on the Altar of the Earth, *Di tan*, just north of the Forbidden City, which was square so as to evoke the terrestrial forces, just as the Round Mound was circular and heavenly; both structures had a stairway leading in each cardinal direction. While the winter Solstice's sacrificial victim was burned so that the smoke could rise to heaven, in summer the sacrifice was buried.

By participating on behalf of humanity in the Earth's natural rhythms, the Emperor aided both the land itself and human society to maintain a healthy balance. His influence was believed to extend even into the cosmos for, in the Chinese system, all things in Heaven and Earth were interconnected and interdependent.

The Chrysanthemum Rising Sun: Japan

Japan's religious and mythic tradition, called Shinto (from the Chinese *shen-tao*, meaning "the way of the higher spirits"), preserves the story of two original ancestors, Izanagi and Izanami, who came down to Earth from Heaven and created the eight islands of Japan and then various deities, including the Sun-goddess Amaterasu. All Japanese Emperors are believed to be direct descendants of Amaterasu and, because of this, Japan is thought to have a unique and divine mission on Earth. All of the Japanese people have a sacred kinship with the Emperor, and the details of their kinship relations with him and thence with various deities comprise a complex ancestor cult.

Japan's astronomy—like so much of her culture—was strongly influenced by China. In the early part of the seventh century a priest named Mim was sent to China to study Buddhism and astronomy. When he returned, he opened Japan's first astronomical observatory at Asuka and founded the Imperial Department of Astronomy, which was charged with the interpretation of unusual celestial events. The Asuka royal astrologers discovered Halley's Comet in October of 684, nearly a millennium before Edmund Halley was born. But the observatory fell into disuse only a few centuries later, and today all that remains are two carved megaliths. One of these stones, weighing 950 tons, is regarded by tradition as having miraculous powers; the second has a series of grooves along its upper surface that point toward the Solstice and Equinox sunset points.

The Japanese New Year was formerly celebrated on *Toji*, the winter Solstice, but now on January 1. Particularly in prewar times, the night before the New Year was marked by the appearance of funerary animals (horses, etc.), and of the gods and goddesses of the spirit world. Secret societies paraded in masks, and troupes of dancers went from house to house rattling bamboo sticks in order to clear out malevolent spirits. Also at this time, the dead were believed to visit the living. It was on the Solstice that Kami reentered the world and gave it new life for the coming year.

Today, the New Year is the most important festival in the Japanese calendar. Arrangements begin many days ahead, with the preparation of special foods and the decoration of houses. Schools close around the time of the December Solstice, and much time is given over to parties. No one works for the first three days of the year, and, in the more traditional families, members exchange gifts and visit shrines.

The Japanese also celebrate the vernal and autumnal Equinoxes. Spring Equinox Day (*Higan*) is a national holiday and the start of a Buddhist festival that celebrates nature and all living things. On Autumn Equinox Day, people customarily visit family graveyards and offer flowers and food to their ancestors.

The Solstices in Vedic India

According to the *Surya Siddhanta*, a Hindu astronomical text, the celestial traditions of India date back to the year 2,163,102 B.C.E. While few modern archaeologists or historians accept this figure as having anything other than mythological significance, it is true nevertheless that Indian astronomy comprises an ancient and complex tradition.

Hindu astronomers were in the habit of discussing enormous time periods—cosmic cycles called *yugas* and *kalpas*—lasting hundreds of thousands, millions, and even billions of years. According to their reckoning, we are now living in the Kali Yuga, which (according to some calculations, at least) began on Friday, February 18th, 3102 B.C.E., and will last another 428,000 years. The Dwapara Yuga, which preceded it, was of twice that duration; and the Treta Yuga, still earlier, lasted three times as long. The first world age of the present series, the Krita Yuga, which was a paradisal Age of Gold in which humans were twenty-one cubits tall and lived four hundred years, was four times the duration of the present Kali Yuga.

But a *kalpa*, according to Brahmagupta, writing in the year 628, lasts a full 4,320,000,000 years—a figure approximating geologists' estimates of the age of the Earth. If we take both the mythic and scientific figures seriously, and if we are indeed nearing the end of a *kalpa*, this could present cause for alarm since, according to tradition, at the end of each *kalpa* the world is destroyed by fire and recreated.

Like their Babylonian and Chinese counterparts, the Brahmin stargazers of ancient India used their celestial observations primarily for astrological purposes. Their cosmology consisted of a flat Earth with a sacred mountain at the center around which the Sun, Moon, and planets orbited—though this picture gradually changed as a result of the introduction of Graeco-Roman astronomical concepts via Alexandria. The Brahmin astronomers noted that the Equinoxes occur at slightly different points of the zodiac each year, but it would be incorrect to say that they discovered the phenomenon of precession since they explained the discrepancy by proposing that the Equinox swings to and fro with a period of seventy-two hundred years.

For the early Indic peoples, as for all ancient cultures, the sky had a profound religious significance. The earliest religious texts of India, the Vedas, which constitute the oldest living religious literature in the world, identify nearly all the major deities with celestial objects. Surya, Vishnu, and Varuna, for example, were all associated with the Sun.

Perhaps the earliest elements of Vedic religious practice consisted of the kindling of sacred fires and the performance of a varied and complex schedule of sacrifices. The purpose of these sacrifices was the reenactment of the creation and the sustenance of the cosmic order. According to P. C. Sengupta, an authority on early Indian astronomy, "The chief requirements for the performance of Vedic sacrifices were to find as accurately as possible the equinoctial and solstitial dates, and thence to find the seasons."[2]

The Hindu calendar has always been based on the cycles of the Moon. Nevertheless, the peoples of many parts of India marked the Solstices and Equinoxes with festivals. For example, northern Indians greeted the winter Solstice with the ceremonial clanging of bells and gongs in order to frighten away hurtful spirits—a custom widespread among all Indo-European peoples.

In the next chapter, we explore Solstice rites that developed among the Indo-Europeans who migrated west and north into Europe. But elements of the same tradition also traveled east and south.

A Solstice Temple in Southeast Asia

Over the course of the last three millennia, the Southeast Asian festival calendar has been influenced by customs imported from Babylonia, China, Muslim Arabia, and India. One example of Hindu influence is the vast temple complex of Angkor Wat in northeast Cambodia, built during the reign of Suryavarman II (C.E. 1113-1150) as a tribute to the god Vishnu. It comprises over two million square meters of temples, walls, galleries, and courtyards, all of which attest to the vision of an architectural genius.

In an article in *Science* in 1976, astronomers Robert Stencel, Fred Gifford, and Eleanor Moro'n reported on the results of their study of maps and charts of Angkor Wat (they were prevented from conducting on-site surveys by the ongoing Cambodian civil war). They concluded that the temple has "calendrical, historical, and mythological data coded into its measurements" and incorporates "built-in positions for lunar and solar observations." They noted also that "the sun was itself so important to the builders of the temple that even the content and position of its extensive bas reliefs are regulated by solar movement." The axis of the complex is oriented in such a way that an observer standing at the western entrance gate can see the Sun rise at the spring Equinox immediately over the central tower of the complex. From the same observing position at the western gate the summer Solstice sunrise occurs directly over the most prominent hill on the horizon, and the winter Solstice sunrise takes place over a small outlying temple 5.5 kilometers southeast of Angkor Wat.

In the traditional Cambodian calendar, the New Year—*Chaul Chham*—commenced around the time of the spring Equinox and

Angkor Wat.

was celebrated by a three-day suspension of normal activities. During the first seven days of the year no living thing could be killed, no business transacted, and no litigation conducted. But the Khmer (ethnic Cambodian) calendar is lunar, and so the timing of the festival in the solar year has shifted somewhat. It is now celebrated in mid-April.

Polynesian Celebrations of Earth and Sky

The wide-ranging Polynesian peoples of the Pacific—inhabiting New Zealand, Hawaii, Tahiti, Samoa, Easter Island, and the Tonga, Cook, and Marquesa Islands, among others—began their migrations from Southeast Asia to Tonga over three thousand years ago. Eastern Polynesia was settled much later, with the first people arriving in the Marquesas, Tahiti, Hawaii, and Easter Island by the year 700, and New Zealand by 1100.

The Polynesians were horticulturalists, cultivating taro, yams, breadfruit, and coconut. They were also, by necessity, keen navigators, whose skills are only now beginning to be understood by scientists. At the time of their first contact with Europeans, they were engaged in planning voyages of up to five hundred miles in length. They found their way from island to island by a thorough understanding of tides, winds, wave patterns, and bird behavior, as well as a detailed knowledge of the stars. Each island was said to be

The stone trilithon at Tonga Tabu, called the Ha'amonga'a (After Childdress)

ruled by particular stars—which meant that from that place, those stars would be seen to pass directly overhead. This was an effective means of determining latitude; once the navigator had steered his vessel to the point at which the proper star passed overhead, all that was left was to set course due east or west toward his destination. The Polynesians visualized the night sky as the ceiling of a great house with rafters and cross beams, with prominent stars at key intersections. Using this mnemonic device, they were able to recall the relative positions of hundreds of stars.

The Polynesians' astronomical interests were not confined to the night sky, nor to the needs of navigation. They noted the seasonal movements of the Sun as well, a practice possibly predating their departure from Asia.

In Tonga, the site of the earliest Polynesian settlements in the Pacific, a huge rough-hewn coral megalithic arch fifteen feet high and eighteen feet long called the *Ha'amonga'a Maui* is aligned to the summer Solstice sunrise. Moreover, a series of grooves on the upper surface of the largest of the stones points to the winter Solstice sunrise. On the winter Solstice (June 21), 1967, king Taufa'ahua Tupou IV observed the sunrise from this spot, confirming the accurate alignment of the marks on the lintel. According to legend, the trilithon was erected by the god Maui with stones from the sea. This, however, is tantamount to a profession of ignorance on the part of the natives, since they are in the habit of attributing to Maui all otherwise unexplainable phenomena.

The Maori of New Zealand personified Heaven and Earth as the sky-god *Rangi nui* and the Earth-goddess *Papa tu a nuku*. It is said that during the year, the Sun roams from Rangi's head to his toes and back again. When the Sun is near Rangi's head, it is summer; when at his feet, it is winter. They also say that when the Sun is near Rangi's head he is spending time with *Hine-raumati*, the Summer Maid. He departs from her in December, however, at the time of the summer Solstice, and heads far out to sea, where lives *Hine-takurua*, the Winter Maid. There the Sun stays until the June winter Solstice, when he heads back toward land.

In Hawaiian mythology, the spirit of the Earth is again called Papa, but the sky is personified as the god *Wakea* (whose name, literally, means *midday*). The two great cosmic principles are also referred to as *Ku* and *Hina*—names and terms that convey much the same meaning as the Chinese *Yang* and *Yin*. Ku and Hina may refer to husband and wife, Heaven and Earth, sunrise and sunset, or generations gone and those yet to come.

The land furthest to the east—that is, toward Ku—in all the Hawaiian Islands is Makapuu Point on Hawaii. There the mythical figure *Kolea-moku* (*muku*) is represented by a red stone at the extreme end of the point. "Two of his wives," according to Martha Beckwith, the great collector of Hawaiian lore,

> also in the form of stones, manipulate the seasons by pushing the sun back and forth between them at the two Solstices. The place is called "Ladder of the sun" and "Source of the sun" and here at the extreme eastern point of land of the whole group, where the sun rises up out of the sea, sun worshipers bring their sick to be healed.[3]

This Hawaiian myth may be the remnant of an elaborate, ancient tradition of astronomical observations and seasonal festivals;

it is impossible to tell. At any rate, the three stones suggest a system of foresights and backsights, such as were commonly used in megalithic Europe and the Americas to determine the times of the Solstices and Equinoxes for the purpose of great communal celebrations.

CHAPTER 7

World Renewal Rites and Myths

IN NEARLY EVERY CULTURE we have surveyed so far, myths and rituals of the Solstices have been focused on the theme of renewal—the renewal of kingship, vegetation, the year, the people, the Sun—indeed, of the world as a whole. In this chapter we explore this theme of renewal in more depth. And since we have yet to sample the Solstice rites of Africa, let us begin with an example from that continent and see how it incorporates the theme.

A World Renewal Rite in Southern Africa

Most of the peoples of central and southern Africa belong to a language group called *Bantu*, a word that, literally translated, means "people," being the combined form of the root *ntu*, "person," and the plural prefix *ba*. There are over four hundred Bantu languages and many more dialects, and the people who speak them pursue a wide diversity of economies and customs. Among the Bantu peoples to have adopted a centralized, monarchical mode of leadership are Swazi, the inhabitants of Swaziland, today a nation bounded by the Republic of South Africa to the north, west, and south, and Mozambique to the east.

Politically, the Swazi are unusual in that their monarchy is dual, being headed both by the king ("The Sun," "The Lion") and the queen mother ("The Earth," "Mother of the Country"). Their society consists of a tightly structured system of clans and lineages, with a highly developed legal system and a wealth of esoteric spiritual traditions. The principal specialists of the society are the diviners (*tangoma*), of whom many are women, whose skills resemble those of Asian shamans, and the medicine men (*inyanga*), who work mostly with the roots, bark, and leaves of local plants to effect their cures.

Traditionally, the most cohesive force in Swazi society was the annual performance of the kingship ceremony, the *Incwala*, which was also the beginning of the year. It was held at the summer (December) Solstice. The rite, according to the Swazi, was aimed at "strengthening the kingship, showing the kingship"; it also served "to make stand the nation."

Anthropologist Hilda Kuper witnessed the ceremonies in the 1930s. She noted that, as the Solstice approached, "throughout the whole country there [was]. . . one main topic of conversation: 'When will the moon and the sun be right?'" Each morning, tribal elders stood in the same spot, facing east, to observe the sunrise against fixed features of the horizon. At the Solstice, the Sun was said to be "resting in its hut," since its rising and setting points remained visibly the same for several days. And each evening they discussed the phase of the Moon and the positions of the stars.

The Swazi believed that the full or waxing Moon brought strength and health, while a person on whom the waning Moon shone would tend toward weakness. It was therefore important that the ceremony coincide not only with the summer Solstice, but with a favorable lunar aspect. Otherwise, the king would not be strong enough to endure the trials of the coming year.

The *Incwala* extended for roughly three weeks in total and was divided into the Little *Incwala*, which lasted two days, and the Big *Incwala*, which lasted six and began on the night of the full Moon.

Ideally, the Little *Incwala* would commence when the Moon was dark, when the king was at his weakest, for part of the ceremony's purpose was to temporarily separate him from society and to make a clean break with the old year. Then, sequestered in his enclosure, he could receive strengthening tonics prepared by his people. But since the new Moon rarely coincides with the exact day of the Solstice, the Swazi sometimes began the ceremony before the arrival of the longest day. Since careful calculations were required, there was always the possibility that an unfavorable day would be chosen, and for the ceremony to be improperly timed would be considered a national calamity, requiring special rituals of cleansing and propitiation.

From the beginning of the ceremony, the king was identified with the Sun. The celebrants—his royal relatives, councilors, and his own regiment of warriors—treated him as though he were powerless and humiliated. In royal homesteads, *Incwala* songs and dances were rehearsed; the words had as their motif the hatred of the king and his rejection by the people.

The Big *Incwala* occurred fourteen days later at the full Moon, when the king would be symbolically reborn and revitalized. On the first day, a regiment of "pure unmarried youths" was sent to obtain branches from a magic tree; these they brought back the second day and presented them to the king's councilors, who used them to enclose the king's sanctuary.

On the third day, the king struck a selected black bull with a rod imbued with the power of fertility and "awakening." Then the pure youths caught and sacrificed the animal. All of this was considered preparation for the fourth, or "Great Day," when the king symbolically overcame the hostility of princely rivals and dispelled the evils and pollution of the past year.

> In the morning he bites "doctored" green foods of the new year; his mothers and others follow suit, their medicines graded by status. Later in the day, under the blazing sun, all the people, in full *Incwala* dress, and with the king in their midst, dance and sing the *Incwala*. Towards sunset the king leaves them; when he re-emerges he is unrecognizable—

a mythical creature—clothed in a fantastic costume of sharp-edged green grass and skins of powerful wild animals, his body gleaming with black unguents. The princes approach and alternately drive him from them into the sanctuary and beseech him to return. Behind them the people sing and dance. . . . Tension mounts as he sways backwards and forwards.[1]

At the climax, the king hurled a specially treated gourd, symbolizing the past year, at his warriors. Then he was led away and his costume removed.

At his hut, the king's ritual wife awaited him, and upon his arrival the couple joined their bodies, symbolically fertilizing the land and the nation.

The king spent the next day in seclusion, his cheeks painted white in imitation of the full Moon, from which he received vitality for the coming year.

On the final day of the *Incwala*, the ritual implements that had been used in the ceremony were symbolically invested with all of the evil of the kingdom and then burned in a great fire. Then the king was publicly bathed, the drops of water falling from his body symbolizing (and magically attracting) the coming rains. The evil and failures of the past year had been driven out, and the forces of life re-energized. As one Swazi put it, "The nation's life, soul, and well-being hang in the faith and belief that the rebirth, rejuvenation, and purification of the king ushers in a new life, added virtue, and strength and national unity."

Though clearly a Solstice world-renewal ceremony, the Swazi *Incwala* possesses many features that seem at first idiosyncratic and unique. But as we will see, most of these features are in fact merely local versions of universal themes and customs that persist down to the present in our own rites. Our route to this realization was paved by the insights of a scholar whose work we must briefly review.

The Golden Bough

Sir James Frazer's *The Golden Bough*, first published in 1890, remains perhaps the most ambitious and influential work ever published on the subject of ancient rites and myths. The editor of an abridged version of the original thirteen-volume work, and a respected mythologist in his own right, Theodor H. Gaster, expresses the opinion that

> what Freud did for the individual, Frazer did for civilization as a whole. For as Freud deepened men's insight into the behavior of individuals by uncovering the ruder world of the subconscious, from which so much of it springs, so Frazer enlarged man's understanding of the behavior of societies by laying bare the primitive concepts and modes of thought which underlie and inform so many of their institutions and which persist, as a subliminal element of their culture, in their traditional folk customs.[2]

Frazer took as his starting point the ancient ceremony for the installation of the priest of the sacred grove of Diana at Aricia, on the shores of Lake Nemi near Rome. "The rule of the shrine was that any man could be its priest, and take the title King of the Wood, provided he first plucked a branch—the Golden Bough—from a certain sacred tree in the temple grove and then killed the priest. This was the regular mode of succession to the priesthood."[3]

Frazer posed two questions: *Why did the new priest have to kill his predecessor?* and *What is the significance of the branch?* His critics asked quite another: Was it really necessary to write thirteen large volumes to solve these riddles? Its detractors have declared *The Golden Bough* "one long, rambling footnote to a line in Ovid. . . ."[4], but in fairness to Frazer it must be emphasized that the story of the priest at Nemi is really only the pretext for a discussion of far wider scope.

In essence, Frazer's argument is this:

The King of the Wood is merely the particular embodiment of the spirit of nature—a formerly universal object of worship. Frazer reasoned that the widespread ancient practice of the ritual sacrifice of a priest or sacred king derived from the belief in the annual sacrifice of a fertility god. It was through the death of the god that new life came to the world. Both the god's death and the rituals celebrating it were associated with seasonally significant dates—

usually, the Solstices. The story of the god's birth, death, and resurrection followed closely the pattern of the Sun's yearly course.

The king also served as the bridegroom of a female spirit, with whom he mated annually to symbolically fecundate the land and people. This sacred marriage, or *hierogamy*, was a widespread custom and correlated with orgiastic practices that accompanied so many of the ancient seasonal festivals.

Ancient agrarian and pastoral societies nearly always associated the vital essence of the king with the health of the kingdom. Thus, if the king showed signs of debility, it was necessary that he be deposed or put to death. In some cases, the old king was removed each year at the time of the Solstice. Often the community would ritually infuse all the noxious influences of the kingdom into the person of the old king, or into some other symbolic scapegoat, whose riddance was thought to cleanse the country.

Between the removal of the old king and the installation of the new, the community enjoyed a period of license. The rules of the society were temporarily suspended and in many cases deliberately transgressed. Masters and servants traded places, and no one worked.

The fertility or power of the land was believed to be embodied not only in the king, but also in certain nonhuman entities, such as certain stones or trees. Especially large, beautiful, unusual, or fortuitously-sited trees were taken as objects of worship. According to Frazer, the oak was particularly venerated in this way, and the custom of either burning a sacred tree or setting one up and decorating it at Midsummer or Midwinter was widespread.

The Dying and Resurrected God

Frazer identified the golden bough itself with the parasitic mistletoe, credited in European folklore with magical properties, especially so if plucked at the Solstice or Equinox since its golden color is supposed to be due to its ability to store up the power of the Sun.

The purpose of the plucking of the bough was to ensure transmission of the indwelling spirit of fertility when, as must have happened in the original form of the rite, the tree itself was felled and burned. That this indeed took place may be inferred from the burning of the Yule log and of lighting fires at such crucial seasons as midsummer and midwinter.[5]

The Scandinavian Norse associated the mistletoe with Balder, their god of poetry and eloquence, son of Frigga and Odin. They regarded Balder as the best of the divinities. The youthful Balder was said to have had a premonition of his own death. Of this he told his mother, who sought the counsel of the other gods. She obtained a promise from fire and water, iron and every other metal, earth and stones, trees, poisons, birds, beast, and sickness of every kind that none would hurt Balder. Since he was now invincible, the gods amused themselves by throwing things at him. But Loki, a divine mischief-maker, disguised himself as an old woman and asked Frigga if indeed *everything* had sworn never to hurt her son. Frigga, in an unwise placement of trust, admitted that in her search she had forgotten to demand an oath from mistletoe. Loki found a mistletoe bough, put it in the hands of the blind god Hoder, and challenged him to hit Balder. Hoder, seeking only to join the fun, hurled the bough and pierced Balder, who fell dead in his tracks. His body was then burned on a pyre and the gods mourned the passing of the brightest and best among them. In some versions of the story, Balder was then brought back to life by his mother's love, her tears becoming crystallized as mistletoe berries. According to tradition, it is because of this victory of love over death that it was divinely ordained that mortals should thenceforth hold mistletoe sacred and that it should never grow on or under the Earth but ever suspended between Earth and Heaven.

Frazer interpreted the story as follows. Ancient peoples must have regarded the mistletoe, which remains green all year round, as the life of the oak—and therefore of the king as well, since the king and the oak, both embodying the life and fertility of the kingdom, are equivalent and interchangeable. The story of Balder is thus to be regarded as the text of a magical Solstice drama in which the king was burned and the mistletoe cut as "a magical rite to cause the sun to shine, trees to grow, crops to thrive, and to guard man and beast from the baleful arts of fairies and trolls, of witches and warlocks."[6] Frazer tied Balder's death to the summer Solstice, when in Scandinavia mistletoe was gathered and bonfires—known in Sweden as "Balder's balefires"—were kindled, representing the god's funeral pyre. Midsummer, after all, is the time when the Sun figuratively begins to "die," commencing its annual sacrifice.

Frazer drew parallels between Balder and other dying-resurrected gods of fertility. One of the oldest of these was the Sumerian Dumuzi, whom the Babylonians called Tammuz. In an early version of the myth, Inanna, the Queen of Heaven, journeys to the underworld, where she dies and is restored to life. But she cannot return to the land of the living without leaving a substitute for herself. The demons of the netherworld attempt to carry off several gods for this purpose, but Inanna rescues each in turn. Finally, she returns home to her son/brother/lover Dumuzi. He fails to humble himself before her, and so she hands him over to the demons. Dumuzi entreats Utu, the Sun god, to save him, but here the text fragment breaks off; we do not know how the story ends.

In later Babylonian versions, the purpose of Inanna's (now Ishtar's) descent to the underworld is to rescue Tammuz, who has died; she succeeds, and he makes a triumphal return to the land of the living. The land has been made desolate by his absence, and by that of Ishtar as well: in "the bull springs not upon the cow; the ass impregnates not the jenny; in the street the man impregnates not the maiden."[7] Gradually, as the old goddess religions were suppressed, Ishtar assumed a more malevolent and secondary role in the myth, while the death and resurrection of Tammuz became the centerpiece. By the time it was carried to other countries, the myth had come to be associated with seasonal rites involving ritual mourning (hence the reference in Ezekiel to the women of Israel weeping for Tammuz) and celebration.

In the Phoenician and Greek form of the myth, the principal characters were Adonis (whose name was simply the Semitic term for "lord") and Aphrodite. While Adonis was still an infant, the goddess Aphrodite hid him in a chest, which she gave to Persephone, goddess of the underworld, for safe keeping. But Persephone opened the chest and, beholding the great beauty of the child, refused to return it to Aphrodite. The two goddesses of love and death fought over Adonis until Zeus finally intervened, declaring that the boy should spend half the year with one, and half with the other. Eventually he was killed by a wild boar—or the jealous Ares in the form of a boar—and was bitterly mourned by Aphrodite. The myth was ritualized and celebrated annually as a festival either at the spring Equinox (as in Phoenicia) or the summer Solstice (as in Attica).

The Egyptians preserved a similar tradition regarding their god Osiris, who was a god of death and resurrection and also of the seasons and vegetation. His myth exists in many versions. Typically, he is described as the son of Heaven and Earth, handsome, and taller than other men. When his father Geb retired to the heavens, Osiris succeeded him as king and took his sister Isis as his queen. He then taught his subjects to abandon cannibalism and to practice the arts of agriculture, winemaking, and music. He was not only a civilizer but an enemy of violence, spreading gentleness and wisdom wherever he went. But Osiris's brother Set was jealous and plotted to gain the kingdom for himself. He organized a band of conspirators who assassinated the beloved ruler and sealed his body in a coffer, which they cast into the Nile.

The coffer was carried out to sea and came to rest on the Phoenician coast at the base of a tamarisk tree, which quickly grew to incorporate the chest within its trunk. As it happened, the king of Byblos ordered that this tamarisk be cut down and used as a column to support the roof of his palace. But the trunk gave off an exquisite scent, which became the subject of discussions that soon reached the ears of Isis who, with her uncommon powers of deduction, immediately understood what had happened. She went to Byblos, was presented with the tree trunk, drew forth the coffer and her husband's body, which she bathed with her tears. But no sooner had she returned the corpse to Egypt than Set gained possession of it and cut it into fourteen pieces, which he scattered far and wide. Isis managed not only to find and rejoin the fragments of Osiris's body (except for one—his phallus), but restored it to eternal life.

The cult of Osiris dominated Egypt for many centuries. Just as human beings could hope for eternal life beyond the grave through Osiris, so through him were the Sun, the plants, and even the Nile annually renewed.

Still another form of the myth of a dying/resurrected god of the seasons was told by the Phrygians of central Turkey. Attis, the protagonist in this version, was a young shepherd of extraordinary beauty such that the monstrous god Agdistis saw and fell in love with him. But Midas, king of Pessinous, sought to separate the youth from the savage deity, and to this end gave the boy Kybele, his daughter, to wed on the vernal Equinox. But Agdistis appeared at the ceremony and drove the wedding party mad with the music of his syrinx (panpipe). In a frenzy, Attis castrated himself next to a pine tree and there bled to death. Violets sprang from the Earth where drops of his blood had fallen. In some versions of the story, the remorseful Agdistis convinces Zeus to bring Attis back to life three days later.

Frazer equated Kybele with Mother Earth. Through Attis's sacrifice in the spring, he fertilizes the Earth with his life blood. And so priests in the service of Kybele ritually castrated themselves and spilled their own blood at the annual rite of the vernal Equinox, reinforcing in this gruesome way the ancient mystical bonds between the Sun, sexuality, and the vitality of the land.

Frazer's work has been both criticized and defended in the decades since its publication. For example, while according to Frazer the dying/resurrected gods represented the vegetation spirit, recent scholarship has tended to see them more generally as embodiments of the divine force that animates the land and the community. The rites are not therefore mere allegories of sowing and reaping but, in the words of Gaster, "are designed rather to account for the rhythm of nature. . . ." Still, as we come to better understand the ancients' attitudes toward Sun, Moon, life, and nature, Frazer's accomplishment in showing the universality and similarity of seasonal rites, and in documenting in vast detail the connections between rite and myth, is certain to be appreciated for many generations to come.

The New Year

In editing and abridging Frazer's thirteen-volume work, Gaster brought a half century of new scholarship to bear on the question of the meaning of the ancient seasonal festivals. He summarized this new information in a series of valuable notes to the text. There, and in his own books and papers, he theorized that the great majority of the rites Frazer had described fit the pattern of what Gaster considered the oldest and most universal of festivals—that of the New Year.

> There is scarcely a people, ancient or modern, savage or civilized, which has not observed it or does not observe it in one form or another. Yet no other festival has been celebrated on so many different dates or in so many seemingly different ways. . . . The more one examines them, however, the clearer does it become that these observances which seem at first sight so different and diverse are really no more than variations upon the same theme; and that though the accompanying emotions may have changed and though he may be completely unconscious of this fact, the behavior of the modern sophisticate on New Year's Eve or New Year's morn stems ultimately from the same roots as does that of his more primitive brethren.[8]

The concept of the year is by no means universal; many ancient peoples, while noting various cycles of nature, nevertheless observed nothing similar to our standard, continuous, twelve-month calendar. Time was conceived in terms of readily observable changes in vegetation, weather, and animal behavior, and the people had little need for a longer, uniform unit. This is true as well for many cultures who celebrated the Solstices and the lunar cycles. The Hopi, for example, had few terms in their language for time intervals, and even the ideas of past, present, and future—so basic to the worldview of speakers of European languages—were alien. According to linguist Helmut Gipper, the Hopi "live in time but not *apart* from it, they are bound up in time but are not neutral observers of objective physical time."[9]

The English term *year* is derived from an Indo-European word that meant "springtime." At some point in the development of civilization, the observation of celestial and terrestrial cycles led to the idea of the annual calendar, and the passionate concern for beginnings and endings with which archaic peoples had regarded the rhythms of nature was transferred to the idea of the year. It is difficult for us in the modern world, who see the New Year merely as a time of fun, frivolity, and hollow resolutions, to appreciate the seriousness with which early peoples regarded the occasion. To them the New Year was the time when the world ended and began again; and in order for the Sun to continue shining, the rain falling, crops growing, and animals reproducing, human beings had to play their ritual part in the cosmic proceedings.

In his book *New Year: Its History, Customs, and Superstitions,* Gaster outlined a four-part program of rites that is typical of nearly all ancient New Year and world renewal ceremonials. This program began with expressions of *Mortification.* As the old year drew to a close, the life of the land and the people was at low ebb. The rites of mortification manifested this condition through fasts and other austerities. No business could be conducted, no marriages performed. The king was ritually deposed or even slain, and a temporary substitute was appointed who held office until the former regent was reinstated or a successor appointed. Often, the days of mortification were considered as not belonging within the calendar; it was as if time itself had ceased.

Having brought itself to a standstill, the community then engaged in rites of *Purgation* as a way of ridding itself of all evil influences. Demons could be exorcised through a variety of means— fires, the ringing of bells, the cleansing of houses and temples with water, the replacement of ritual objects. Often a human or animal scapegoat was invested with all of the evil and contagion of the community and driven beyond its borders.

Having purified itself, the community then undertook rites of *Invigoration*—positive procedures for the renewal of life. These might take the form of mock combat between the forces of Life and Death, Summer and Winter, Rain and Drought, Old Year and New, represented by individuals or teams. More commonly, the reinvigoration of the land and people was accomplished through the deliberate release of sexual energy. The king led this purposeful discharge of passion in a symbolic sacred wedding with a temple votaress.

Finally, all joined in celebratory rites of *Jubilation*. Anxiety gave way to relief, and the community engaged in feasts and merriment. The forces of life had once again prevailed, and the ancient bonds of society and nature had been re-established.

We have already explored three examples of Gaster's prototypical New Year rite—the Babylonian *Akitu*, the Swazi *Incwala*, and the Incan *Inti Raymi*—all related to the Solstices or Equinoxes. The Sioux Sun Dance and the Chinese Solstice rites, though they did not occur at the beginning of the calendar year, also somewhat fit the pattern.

The New Year has not always been celebrated on the Solstices or Equinoxes. All ancient cultures faced the problem of reconciling the cycle of the Moon with that of the Sun, and many adopted lunar or semi-lunar calendars. The Jews, for example, begin their civil year at the new Moon of Nisan, preceding the vernal Equinox; while their religious year is measured from the new Moon of Tishri, preceding the autumnal Equinox. The Islamic calendar is completely lunar, so that the months rotate through the seasons of the year; the New Year festival, *Muharram*, occurs eleven days earlier each year in relation to the Equinoxes and Solstices. The Creeks, Cherokees, and Choctaws of North America began their year with the full Moon in late summer. And the Chinese started the New Year with the new Moon closest to the beginning of spring.

Nevertheless, the nations that have observed a solar calendar have nearly all settled on a Solstice or Equinox as its beginning. Medieval Europe took December 25 as the beginning of the year; then, from about the end of the Middle Ages and until recent times, the New Year was celebrated on the vernal Equinox. France changed to January 1 in 1564; Holland in 1575; Scotland in 1660; Protestant Germany in 1700; Russia in 1706; England in 1752; and Sweden in 1753.

Other peoples (some of whom we have already surveyed) like the Chumash, the Hopi, and the Inuit of Hudson Bay in America;

the shamanistic Koryaks of Siberia; and the East Greenlanders, all looked to the winter Solstice as the beginning of the year. And, as we have seen, the Swazi began the year with the summer Solstice.

Our own present calendar, which is of Roman origin, begins, of course, on January 1. The early Romans had celebrated the New Year in March, at the time of the vernal Equinox; but there can be little doubt that, when they changed their calendar to begin on January 1, they were aiming at the winter Solstice. When Julius Caesar instituted his reformed Republican calendar in the year we call 46 B.C.E., he retained the then-traditional New Year date of January 1, which by that time had wandered from the true date of the Solstice by nearly a full season.

Julius added ninety days to the year 46 B.C.E., so that January 1 of 45 B.C.E. occurred seven days after the winter Solstice, which fell on or about December 25. But, owing to the inaccuracy of the Julian calendar, the New Year and the Solstice continued to move apart, so that by the time of the Gregorian reform in 1582, the latter had slipped to its present date of about December 21 (in the northern hemisphere).

The word *January* derived from the name of the god Janus, which in turn derived from *janua*, meaning "door." Because a door permits movement both in and out, Janus was portrayed as having two faces—one looking forward, the other back. For the Romans, as for every people, the New Year was a time to dissipate the accumulated ills of the past seasons and to infuse their world with renewed energy for the cycle to come.

The Roman festival of world renewal was *Saturnalia*, named after the god Saturn (Greek: *Kronos*), who had been king of the world during the mythic Golden Age. That was a time before agriculture, when humanity lived in friendship with the animals, without war or private property. Saturnalia was the greatest festival of the year in Imperial Rome, and was celebrated in December, in the days leading up to the Solstice and the New Year. In its overturning of social norms, it was yet another example of Gaster's prototypical New Year rite. During Saturnalia, according to Frazer,

The distinction between the free and the servile classes was temporarily abolished. The slave might rail at his master, intoxicate himself like his betters, sit down at table with them, and not even a word of reproof would be administered to him for conduct which at any other season might have been punished with stripes, imprisonment, or death. Nay, more, masters actually changed places with their slaves and waited on them at table; and not until the serf had done eating and drinking was the board cleared and dinner set for his master.[10]

The King of Saturnalia was chosen by lot, and presided over the revels, issuing playful and ludicrous commands to his temporary subjects. In a few districts, the mock king ended his reign by cutting his own throat on the altar of the god Saturn, having taken on himself the offenses of the community.

In other respects, the occasion was a uniformly happy one. Presents were given, people dressed in costumes and finery, school was suspended, feasts were held, evergreens were used for decoration, war was delayed, and sexual liberties were indulged. While the festival eventually earned a reputation for licentiousness and drunkenness, Saturnalia was originally intended to memorialize the historically real time before the invention of laws and property, when all people were equal and lived close to nature.

We began this chapter with a look at an African Solstice rite, the *Incwala* of the Swazi, and ended with the Roman festival of *Saturnalia*. While Imperial Rome and Swaziland might appear at first to have little in common culturally, a comparison of the two rites shows several similarities. Both centered on a dying-resurrected king. Both aimed to fertilize the kingdom, and did so through dance and orgiastic sexuality. Both occurred on or around a Solstice. And both served ritually to rid the community of the evil of the past year. As we see in the next chapter, residues of all of these elemental ritual themes live on into the present.

CHAPTER 8

The Solstices in Europe

AS WE HAVE JUST SEEN, the ancient Romans celebrated the winter Solstice on the 25th of December, the day following the culmination of Saturnalia. It was only natural that they should so emphasize the Solstice in their calendar, given the importance of the Sun in their state religion.

Sol, the Sun god, had an ancient cult in Rome dating perhaps to Etruscan times. In about 10 B.C.E., Augustus replaced Sol in the official observances with the Greek deity Apollo (who had his own solar associations), but as the Empire's borders lumbered eastward, it was inevitable that Syrian and Iranian Sun-worship would revive Rome's indigenous counterpart. Around the year 200, the Emperor Severus identified himself with Sol and took the title INVICTUS (unconquered), an epithet already commonly applied to the Sun. His reasons for doing so were largely political. The Empire by that time embraced a multitude of languages, tribes, and ethnic religions; and so a rallying-point was needed. Moreover, many of the Emperors had conducted themselves so foolishly or cruelly that the common people found it difficult to take seriously the official dogma that the Emperor was an incarnate deity. The Sun, being inherently worthy of worship, served as an ideal symbol around which to consolidate the temporal and religious power of the state. Thus in the year 274, the Emperor Aurelian chose December 25—the traditional winter Solstice date—as the festival day for Sol Invictus.

One of the imported religions that was gaining a large following in Rome at the time was the Iranian cult of Mithras. According to legend, Mithras had been sent to Earth by the supreme God of Light to slay a great bull whose blood was the source of all fertility. Only men (most of them Roman soldiers) participated in Mithraic rites. Neophytes were required to undergo baptism and to perform deeds of self-sacrifice and courage, thereby progressing through seven stages of initiation. The process was said to bring about a gradual purification of character, leading finally to the unconditioned state that the soul had known before birth. Having achieved this seventh degree, the initiate was regarded as an incarnation of the divine.

The central event of the cult myth, the slaying of the cosmic bull, was regarded as the greatest event in the history of the world— the act of Creation at the beginning of time, and of redemption at its end. Believers reenacted the drama in a nocturnal bull sacrifice in a cave or grotto. This ceremony was seen as a celebration of the union of opposites—life and death, spring and autumn, beginning and ending. Sculptures and paintings of the bull slaying showed grain flowing from the wound in the animal's neck.

Mithras's birth was supposed to have been attended by shepherds. At the end of his time on Earth he and his disciples shared a last supper, which was later commemorated by believers in a communion of bread and wine. Further, the hero was said not to have died but to have returned to heaven, and his followers believed that he would come again at the end of the world. Then the dead would rise from their graves for a final judgment.

The Mithraic holy day was Sun-day, a fact no doubt noted by Emperor Aurelian, who, with so many of his soldiers being initiated into the Iranian cult, must have wondered: Why not consolidate the worship of Mithras with that of Sol Invictus? Accordingly, he declared December 25th the official birth festival not only of Sol, but of Mithras as well.

By the fourth century, a radical Jewish sect calling themselves Christians was brewing trouble for the Roman authorities. The Emperor Constantine, realizing that the best way to defuse the movement might be to co-opt it, made Christianity the state religion with himself as its head. The Christians went along, though doing so entailed a few revisions to their rites and beliefs. Previously their Sabbath was Saturn-day; but for unity's sake, Constantine changed it to Sun-day, the feast day of both Sol and Mithras. This was acceptable to Christians since, after all, Christ's resurrection had occurred on a Sunday, the day after the Jewish Sabbath (Saturday) following the Passover.

Moreover, within another quarter of a century or so (by the year 360, certainly) the December 25 feast-day of Sol and Mithras had become the principal Christian festival as well, the day for the commemoration of the birth of Jesus. This date met with the approval of Christians because, first of all, no one knew Jesus's real birthday anyway; and second, because the winter Solstice had always been seen as a time of renewal. It was the time of the rebirth of the Sun and of light. Therefore how fitting to use it as the day to celebrate the birth of the true spiritual light of the world! And, even though the Solstice ceased to occur on December 25 centuries ago due to calendrical inaccuracies, Christians have celebrated Christmas on this day in every year since.

In doing so, they have, as we see shortly, perpetuated rites and customs that have much more to do with the ancient festivals, and particularly Solstice festivals, than with the historical Jesus or with Christian doctrine. Throughout the Middle Ages, the adoption of pagan festivals into the Christian calendar continued, following a typical pattern of initial violent suppression of indigenous rites followed by co-optation—a strategy not unlike that used by Imperial Rome against Christianity itself. It was by this means that the Celtic worship of the Earth Goddess would become the cult of the Virgin Mary, and the celebration of the Resurrection would come to be called Easter—after Eostre, a Greek goddess of fertility and light.

The story of the violent putting down of the old folkways by the representatives of the Church, at first in Europe and then throughout the Americas, Africa, Asia, and Australasia, is one that deserves a detailed accounting, which it has received elsewhere.[1] But the people's continuing loyalty to the old traditions is epitomized in the many European medieval church basilicas that were oriented by their master builders to the solsticial sunrise points. The twelfth-century Romanesque basilica of Vezelay, France, is one example. There, at winter Solstice, sunlight streams through the upper windows of the nave and directly illuminates the upper capitals of the column; at summer Solstice, according to William Marlin, sunlight "streams down into the nave and creates footprints of itself precisely down the middle."[2]

Survivals of Ancient Festivals in Christmas Customs

In the Roman calendar, the first day of each month was called the *Kalends* (the word from which, of course, we derive our word *calendar*). The Kalends of January, being the start of the New Year, was the occasion for great festivities. The following description of these January Kalends revels, by the Greek sophist Libanius of the fourth century, has been quoted by several authors of books on the origins of Christmas customs, for obvious reasons:

> The impulse to spend seizes everyone...People are not only generous themselves, but also towards their fellowmen. A stream of presents pours itself out on all sides...the Kalends festival banishes all that is connected with toil, and allows men to give themselves up to undisturbed enjoyment. From the minds of young people it removes two kinds of dread: the dread of the schoolmaster and the dread of the stern pedagogue...Another great quality of the festival is that it teaches men not to hold too fast to their money, but to part with it and let it pass into other hands.

The Scandinavian word *Yule* (Danish *Jul*) long ago came to denote Christmas, and is so used today in English-speaking and northern European countries. Its derivation is uncertain, though it may come from the Anglo-Saxon word *hweol*, or "wheel," referring perhaps to the course of the Sun through the Solstices and Equinoxes. In any case, many historians have suggested that the term originally may have designated a Teutonic Solstice festival. Perhaps the twelve nights of Yule festivities coincided with the twelve days when the Sun's rising and setting points seemed to "stand still" at the southern extreme on the horizon.

The Germanic peoples had marked their seasonal festivals with fires, dancing, and sacrifices. The fires of the winter Solstice were thought to promote the return of the Sun, to burn away the accumulated misdeeds of the community, and to ward off evil spirits. The tradition of the burning of a special log (the Yule log) on Christmas Eve was practiced throughout Europe, from Scandinavia to Italy. Indeed, the words for Christmas among the Lithuanians and Letts literally signify "Log Evening." The Yule log was in some places considered the Fire Mother of the Sun god. In parts of Germany it was the custom to place a large block of wood on the fire and then to take it out before it was consumed, preserving it throughout the year for its magical protective properties. Its ashes were buried beneath fruit trees or used to rid cattle of vermin or to protect houses from lightning.

In England and Scandinavia the Yule Log was often replaced by a large candle, which was intended to burn throughout the entire day. For the candle to go out for any reason was considered a portent of death or ill luck. The wax from the candle was held to have magical properties, particularly when smeared on a plow the following spring or when fed to birds.

In preindustrial England local communities would elect a whimsical, semi-official personage called the "Lord of Misrule" to preside over Christmas festivities. This pseudo-potentate was allowed a certain amount of license even in the royal household, and in the houses of the nobles he held court at banquets and games. Among the lower ranks the institution of the Lord of Misrule was not only a source of mirth and mischief in general, but a way of poking fun at the nobility. The person elected to this position generally indulged in every sort of prank, the wilder the better, often sending his subjects on impossible errands or mercilessly satirizing the temporal and religious authorities—all with impunity. John Stubbs, in his sixteenth-century *Anatomie of Abuses*, wrote disapprovingly:

The wilde heades of the parish, flocking together chuse them a graund captaine of mischief, whom they innoble with the title of My Lord of Misrule. They marche these heathen compaine towards the church and churchyard, their pipers pyping, drummers thonderying, their stumpes dauncing, their belles jyngling, their handkerchefes swyngyng about their heads like madmen, their hobbie-horses and other monsters skyrmishing amongst the throng. . . .

The Lord of Misrule was, of course, a throwback to the King of Saturnalia. In England as in Rome, he offered nobles and commoners alike a chance to lampoon the conventions of society, recalling a bygone age of innocence in which all had been free and equal.

Later, Oliver Cromwell in England and Cotton Mather in Massachusetts would forbid the celebration of Christmas altogether. Mather was incensed by all the "revelling, dicing, carding, masking, mumming." In his time, the people of New England were prohibited by law from openly observing the day. The ordinance was repealed in 1681.

The Sacred Tree

"From the earliest times," wrote Frazer, "the worship of trees has played an important part in the religious life of European peoples." Nearly all of Europe was formerly one great primeval forest (of which only a few square miles in Poland today remain). The divine, in all its myriad forms, was sung and danced and prophesied in sacred groves; Teutonic and Druidic temples were natural woods. Trees themselves were regarded as full of spirit, and many ancient peoples felled living trees only out of great necessity. The Dyaks, Chinese, Ojibways, Abyssinians, and New Guineans (among many others) all had traditions forbidding the harming of green or fruit-bearing trees, believing that the tree—no less than an animal or a human being—feels pain, bleeds, and utters cries of indignation. Moreover, it was believed possible for the spirit of a person to animate a tree.

Some of this regard for trees survived until quite recent times. In Sweden, well into the last century, nearly every farm still had an ancestral tree whose growth and well-being were a barometer for the health of all that grew on the farm.

Back in the days when Europe was inhabited by wandering tribes, it was their custom to build settlements in groups, with one in the center called the "mother town." And at the center of each clearing they left a clump of trees, dominated by a particularly large or beautiful example known as the "mother tree."

Both the ancient Norse and the people of Central Asia envisioned the Universe as a great tree, with the Earth's axis as its trunk. The stars were lights in its branches, the underworld lay among its roots. Similar world-tree ideas are to be found among the native peoples of North America, and those of India and China as well.

The first Christmas tree is associated by legend with St. Boniface (earlier known as Wynfred) and his conversion of the Germanic peoples to Christianity. As the story goes, a local chieftain named Gundhar was about to sacrifice his own eldest son to the gods on Christmas Eve. A great oak, sacred to the Norse deity Thor, was to be the scene of this act. Boniface strove to prevent the sacrifice by destroying the tree, thus proving the pagan god powerless. But, after only one stroke of his axe, a great wind came up and toppled the oak. The assembled throng was suitably awed and asked Boniface for the word of God. Pointing to a little fir growing close by, he told them it was the holy tree of the Christ child. "Gather about it, not in the wild woods but in your homes," Boniface is reputed to have said. "There it will shelter no bloody deeds, but loving gifts and lights of kindness." The story, which is almost universally acknowledged as apocryphal, must have served as a useful bit of propaganda in persuading generations of Europeans to give up their ancient traditions of tree worship, by preserving a residue of that tradition in an innocuous, Christianized form.

According to another legend, Martin Luther was wandering about on Christmas Eve beneath a clear sky full of shining stars. When he returned home, he brought with him a young fir tree, which he set up and lit with little candles in order to remind his children how Christ, the light of the world, had so gloriously brightened the sky on the first Christmas Eve.

Legend aside, the real story of the origin of the Christmas tree, though lost to history, probably derives from both Christian and non-Christian customs. Evergreen trees and wreaths had been used by the Romans in their Saturnalia and Kalends winter Solstice festivals for centuries. Garlands of yew, juniper, laurel, and pine, all prized for their beauty and fragrance, decorated homes and public places. Rosemary, an evergreen shrub sometimes called the "herb of the Sun," was especially favored at the winter Solstice. And in medieval times, a Paradise play—featuring Adam, Eve, the serpent, and two trees—was performed on Christmas Eve. Legend had it that when Adam left Eden, he took with him a sprout of the Tree of Knowledge, from which sprang the tree of whose wood Christ's cross was built. This Paradise tree has often been mentioned as a possible forerunner of the Christmas tree.

Though it is somewhat futile to search back in history for the "first Christmas tree," it is possible to trace notable turning points in the evolution of the ceremonial evergreen—in seventeenth-century Germany, with the first written descriptions of "fir trees set up in the rooms of Strasbourg and hung with roses cut from paper of many colors, apples, wafers, spangle-gold, sugar, etc."; in England in 1840, when the German Prince Albert set up a tree in the palace for his wife, Queen Victoria; and across the Atlantic in 1845, when a children's book, *Kriss Kringle's Christmas Tree*, which has been described as the most influential Christmas book in the United States, spread the fashion throughout America.

The Solstice Shaman

The origin of that other venerable fixture of Christmas, Santa Claus, is somewhat better known. Again the light of pagan traditions shines dimly in the background of modern custom.

The name Santa Claus is derived from Saint Klaus (Dutch: *Sinter Klaas*), the Germanic equivalent of Saint Nicholas. The known historical facts about the Turkish St. Nicholas, the fourth-century Bishop of Myra, are sketchy at best, though he was apparently famous for his anonymous generosity, especially to young people. It was probably for this reason that he later became the patron saint of boys. At any rate, legend has it that one night he put money into the stockings of the daughters of a poor nobleman. Gradually, the festivities of St. Nicholas's Day, December 6, came to be transferred to the season of Christmas, and in the Germanic countries, children came to associate the gray-bearded, robed, and mitred figure with the festivities of Christmas Eve.

The modern picture of Santa derives from other sources as well. Knecht Ruprecht, a legendary Germanic personage, was said to travel from town to town on Christmas clad in skins and straw, testing children's knowledge of their prayers. If they passed his examination, he rewarded them with fruit, nuts, and gingerbread, which he carried in a sack; for those not so diligent, he brandished a punishing rod.

In England, as early as the fourteenth century, Christmas mummer's plays featured a white-bearded old gent wearing a wreath of holly. But Father Christmas, as he was known, though jolly enough, had none of the magical qualities of the reindeer-herder so beloved by children today. That character is more a creature of literature than of folklore.

It is to Washington Irving that we owe the amalgamation of earlier traditions into the composite figure of the modern Santa Claus. In his 1809 *Father Knickerbocker's History of New York*, Irving describes Santa riding over rooftops in his sleigh, putting his finger to the side of his nose, and bringing gifts to good children.

While this familiar image of Santa Claus may have a fairly recent origin, the idea of a kindly, bearded man living at the North Pole and flying magically around the world resonates with cultural traditions that are far more ancient.

Christmas, as we have seen, had been associated from the beginning with the winter Solstice—a time when the shamans and priests of cultures throughout the world officiated at rites of world renewal. And the theme of renewal inevitably lent itself to the recollection and celebration of that original Paradise or Golden Age, when nature, cosmos, and humankind existed together in perfect harmony. These associations are clear in an old Serbian belief that at midnight on Christmas Eve the world is grafted onto Paradise, and in a Breton tradition, that on Christmas Eve the animals can speak (a power they are supposed to have possessed in the Golden Age, according to many cultures' accounts). Kronos, the King of the World during the Golden Age according to the ancient Greeks, was alleged by some authors to have lived at the North Pole. And shamans from Australia to Africa, and from Asia to America, were thought to have been capable of flying through the air and of moving at will among the various spiritual and material realms of existence.

When we add these elements together, we begin to see that, while it is impossible to trace any direct connection between the shamanic tradition and Santa Claus, his appeal may nonetheless draw upon collective memories and beliefs reaching back perhaps even to Paleolithic times. E. C. Krupp writes:

> If a cosmic tree points the way to heaven for us every Christmas, Santa Claus undertakes the magical flight of a shaman. He is sometimes said to be responsible for erecting the Christmas tree sky pole himself. Descending vertically down the chimney, Santa returns by the same route back to the roof. Our chimneys, like the cosmic axis, carry him from one realm to another. There must also be something magical about the sack he carries, for it can supply toys to all of the children in the world. That bag is like the *sampo* or the magic mill that could grind out unlimited supplies of food, money, and salt and was associated with the World Axis. In addition, Santa Claus, like the gods and spirits, is immortal. His activity is focused on that critical night that was once the winter solstice.[3]

And so we have the modern Christmas celebration, most elements of which (with the exception of those few that are focused specifically on the biblical stories of the birth of Jesus) have been derived from ancient festivals, traditions, and beliefs having to do with sacred trees, world renewal, shamanic ecstasy, and the seasonal dance of Earth and Sun. Christmas supplanted the Solstice by absorbing its superficial emblems while ignoring or suppressing many of its central meanings.

But now that we know more about ancient and tribal peoples, many Christians are realizing that little of the content of the old celebrations actually contradicts the *spirit* of their own faith. After all, Jesus said nothing about eradicating ancient festivals. He was a lover of nature who enjoined his followers to come as little children and to imitate the flowers and the birds by taking no thought for tomorrow, laying up no earthly treasure. Indeed, two of the most sensitive and thoughtful modern Christian theologians, Matthew Fox and Thomas Berry, are advocating a return to the values inherent in the ancient nature religions as a way both to save the ecology of planet Earth and to bring new relevance to the institution of the church.

Perhaps there will come a time when religious paranoia and the ethic of conquest will at last give way to humility before life itself—an attitude that has been modelled and preached by virtually every spiritual teacher in history. When that day arrives, we may find much to celebrate in the simple but profound messages that plants and animals, Earth and Sky have to offer.

The Summer Solstice: Midsummer's Day

If winter Solstice, as the symbol of death and rebirth, is an occasion of hope, the summer Solstice is fulfillment tinged with sadness. It is a time of abundance, warmth, and fertility. The nights are short and the days long; nature is at her peak. And yet from this moment onward until Midwinter, light will retreat and darkness will increase, until the promise of spring and the plenitude of summer have fully given way to the bitter-sweet scents of autumn and the first frost of winter.

But while winter Solstice traditions persist, disguised as Christmas and New Year, the ancient rites of summer Solstice have virtually disappeared from the modern European-American culture, and this despite the fact that, in ancient times, it was often the summer Solstice that was the more prominent. Midsummer's Day has become the forgotten and neglected festival. Why?

From an economic-historical perspective, the answer is simple. Like Midwinter, the summer Solstice was long ago incorporated into the Christian calendar, in this case as the feast day of St. John the Baptist. As John was the forerunner and prophet of Jesus, so does Midsummer foretell the eventual arrival of the seasonal turn of Midwinter. Pius Parsch, in *The Church's Year of Grace*, calls St. John's Day part of the "basic structure of the church year. . . . It is a kind of advent. . . a joyous anticipation of the approaching salvation."[4] But with the flourishing of the industrial age, with its accelerating labor requirements and general pace, all of the saints' days tended to be forgotten. In Medieval times, the calendar included as many as 150 festivals. Now, workers are granted barely a dozen official holidays in the year. Of these, most are secular in origin; only Christmas and Easter, among the Christian feast days, are of sufficient importance to command official holiday status.

But from a perspective that recognizes deeper shifts in the mythic center of gravity of cultures, there is perhaps another reason for the obliteration of the Midsummer rites. The winter Solstice was nearly always regarded as a festival of sky and Sun, and of the divine masculine principle; while the summer Solstice was a festival of the Earth and of the divine feminine. It is now widely acknowledged that Western civilization has systematically suppressed the feminine and plundered the Earth while exalting the masculine and forcibly promoting sky-god religions. No wonder, then, that the great Earth festivals—including not only Midsummer, but May Day and the Full Moon celebrations—have passed into oblivion, as far as the average person is concerned. For those with some interest in redressing our culture's denigration of the feminine, and its calculatedly utilitarian attitude toward the world of nature, the recovery of Midsummer observances must therefore be of special interest.

The Flowers of Midsummer

In pre-industrial Europe most healers were women and most folk-healing was done with herbs. Women's traditional connections with the plant kingdom date back to Paleolithic times, when men began to specialize in the perilous and glorious career of hunting, leaving their mothers, sisters, wives, and daughters to satisfy the bulk of the group's needs through the gathering of wild leaves, roots, seeds, and fruits. And just as men developed magical rites to appease, thank, and influence the animal spirits, women evolved intuitive ties with—and immense practical knowledge of—herbs, knowledge which they passed from generation to generation, mother to daughter. This lore included methods for collecting and extracting natural herbal painkillers, tonics, antispasmodics, and remedies for fevers, indigestion, contraception, and infections.

In the twelfth century, Hildegard of Bingen wrote a manual of herbal and other natural healing methods titled *Liber Simplicis Medicinae*; in it, she listed the healing properties of 213 plants and 55 trees. The book was to become the basis for modern western herbalism and medicine. Shortly after its publication, however, the Inquisition began, during the course of which up to nine million women were executed for "witchcraft"—which often simply meant *the knowledge and practice of the traditional ways of healing*.

The summer Solstice, as the time of the year when the feminine Earth energies are at their height, was also, according to Frazer, "the day of all days for gathering the wonderful herbs by means of which you could combat fever, cure a host of diseases, and guard yourself against sorcerers and their spells."[5] Frazer cites dozens of plant-related traditions tied to the ritual observance of Midsummer; but these are likely only the merest remnants of the ancient lore that must have existed prior to the Inquisition.

Mugwort, known in France as the herb of St. John, was gathered at the summer Solstice and made into garlands or girdles (St. John was supposed to have a worn a girdle of mugwort in the wilderness). It is a tall plant with purplish stems and smooth, dark green leaves with a cottony underside. Herbalists still use mugwort for rheumatism, as a stimulant and nervine tonic, for fevers and ague. Its dried leaves, sown into a pillow, are said to induce particularly vivid dreams.

Vervain is found growing by roadsides and in sunny pastures. It was gathered after sunset on Midsummer's Eve and steeped overnight in water, or dried, or bruised and worn around the neck.

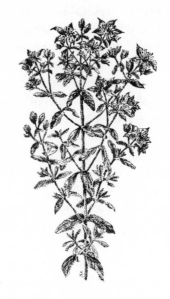

Viscum album (Mistletoe)

Hypericum perforatum (St. John's Wort)

Verbena officinalis (Vervain)

Artemisia vulgaris (Mugwort)

The ancients regarded vervain as an aphrodisiac; they also used it in their sacrifices (its Latin name, *Verbena*, was the term for "altar-plants" in general). Druids, magicians, and sorcerers valued it as highly as did herbal healers—the latter for its astringent, diaphoretic, and antispasmodic properties. It is said to be useful for strengthening the nervous system while relieving stress.

St. John's wort, with its cheery yellow flowers, blooms around the time of the summer Solstice, when it was customarily gathered. Frazer notes that "with its bright yellow petals and masses of golden stamens it might well pass for a tiny copy on earth of the great sun which reaches its culminating point in heaven at this season."[6] Its botanical name *Hypericum* derives from a Greek word meaning "over an apparition," referring to the belief that the plant was so abhorrent to evil spirits that a mere whiff would send them fleeing. It has a sedative and pain reducing, anti-inflammatory effect. Appropriately enough, its oil is said to be useful for the healing of sunburn.

The root of *Mouse-ear Hawkweed* was once thought to yield the blood of St. John. The milky, reddish juice of this chickory-family plant has sudorific, tonic, and expectorant properties, and has been used as a remedy for whooping cough and diseases of the lungs.

At midnight on Midsummer's Eve *Ferns* were once believed to bloom, and soon afterward to seed. Whoever caught the bloom was supposedly endowed thereby with miraculous knowledge and power. But the gatherer must take care not to touch with their hand the magical flower lest it vanish like mist. Each of the many varieties of fern—Male Fern, Shield Fern, Lady Fern, Spleenwort, Wall Rue, Maidenhair, Hart's Tongue, Bracken, etc.—has unique medicinal properties.

Throughout Europe, there was a tradition that a branch of *Hazel* cut on the eve of the summer Solstice would serve as an ideal divining rod for the discovery of water and treasures. Other herbs associated with Midsummer include *Camomile, Geranium, Thyme, Rue, Chervilseed, Giant-fennel,* and *Penny-royal,* all of which were prized for the aromas they exuded when thrown upon bonfires, which were everywhere a signal feature of Midsummer festivals.

The Fires of Midsummer

In her book *Earth Wisdom*, Dolores LaChapelle describes an experience that contributed to her emerging awareness of the nature and significance of the ancient seasonal festivals:

> Some years ago, while climbing in Europe, we stayed at a hut in order to climb the Matterhorn. We happened to be there on the summer solstice. All the climbers in the hut went outside just at dusk and waited expectantly in the gathering twilight. Then far on a distant mountain we saw a fire suddenly blaze up. Then our hutmaster lit the fire at our hut and soon, far down the valley, another fire was lit. It was a moving ceremony there in the wilderness of snow and rock. I asked the hutmaster and the Swiss climbers what it meant. They said, "That's what we always do on St. John's Eve."[7]

What LaChapelle observed in Switzerland was a modern survival of one of the most universal of ancient Midsummer rites. Frazer devoted many pages in *The Golden Bough* to examples of these rites, and called the summer Solstice not only the principal Indo-European fire festival but "the most widely diffused and the most solemn of all the yearly festivals celebrated by the primitive Aryans in Europe."[8]

A sixteenth-century poem by Thomas Kirchmeyer describes the fire festival of his time:

> And yong men round about with maides, doe daunce in every
> streete,
> With garlands wrought of Motherwort, or else with Vervain
> sweete,
> And many other flowres faire, with Violets in their handes,
> Whereas they all do fondly thinke, that whosoever standes,
> And thorow the flowres beholds the flame, his eyes shall feele
> no paine.
> When thus till night they daunced have, they though the fire
> amaine

With striving mindes doe runne, and all their hearbes they cast
therein.
And then with wordes devout and prayers, they solemnly begin,
Desiring God that all their illes may there consumed bee,
Whereby they thinke through all that yeare from Agues to be
free.[9]

Summer Solstice bonfires were kindled in Denmark and Norway, where they were supposed to banish sickness from cattle. In Austria, the people hurled burning discs into the air. The Germans, holding to the same tradition represented in the poem above, wore chaplets of mugwort and vervain and looked into the fire through branches of larkspur, in the belief that this would maintain the health of their eyes. As they left the fire, they threw their herbs on the coals, saying, "May my ill-luck depart and be burned with these."

In Bohemia, boys went from house to house collecting sticks and brush, while girls made wreaths and nosegays. Later, girls and boys would stand on opposite sides of the fire they had built, looking at one another through the wreaths to see whether they would be true to each other and who would marry whom. The girls then threw the wreaths across the flames, each to her sweetheart. When the flames were low enough, each couple joined hands and leapt three times across the fire. The singed wreaths served as a protection from sickness and thunderstorms throughout the following year.

In the British Isles, Midsummer bonfires were lit in all the areas where the old Celtic traditions held sway—in Ireland, Wales, and Cornwall, as well as throughout much of the English countryside. In Scotland, cowherds carrying torches walked three times around their folds, following the course of the Sun, in order to purify and protect the animals.

In Spain, at San Pedro Manrique, the people still build a bonfire at around six P.M. on Midsummer's Eve. By midnight its coals have been spread into a glowing carpet ten feet long and several inches deep, which barefooted men and women walk across, each carrying another person on his or her back. There is silence as each person sets out across the coals, cheering as each finishes. "No clergy are present," writes Jacqueline Simpson, in her account in *European Mythology*,

> possibly as a sign of disapproval, but everyone else is there, led by the Mayor and Council and three elaborately costumed girls called Móndidas ('Pure Ones') chosen by lot from among young local virgins. Early next morning, St. John's Day, the Móndidas take heavy baskets of ornamental loaves to church to be blessed, and then carry them round the town on their heads. Meanwhile, the Mayor and Council circumambulate the town walls and then preside at horse races in the square. At noon, the Móndidas bring the loaves back to the church, where everyone hears High Mass. In the afternoon, the Móndidas recite a long patriotic poem about a defeat of the Moors in 844 A.D., and the rest of the day is spent in dancing.[10]

The custom of lighting bonfires at Midsummer is far from being confined merely to Europe. It was also common in North Africa, which is remarkable because (as we have already noted) the Islamic calendar is entirely lunar and independent of the turn of the seasons. This suggests that the North Africans' Midsummer festivals long predate these people's adoption of Islam.

June Solstice rites were indigenous to the Americas, as we saw in an earlier chapter; but the invading Europeans brought their own customs, which they superimposed on native ones. In Brazil, the practice of leaping over the fires of St. John became commonplace, and Frazer wrote of La Paz, Bolivia that "the Indians of the neighborhood take a pride in kindling bonfires on heights which might seem inaccessible"; then "the darkness of night is suddenly and simultaneously lit up by hundreds of fires, which cast a glare on surrounding objects producing an effect at once weird and picturesque."[11]

Midsummer's Bride

As the time of the year when nature exudes her abundance, the summer Solstice is inevitably and intuitively associated with fertility and sexuality by people everywhere. June is still the most popular month for weddings, even though most cultures have forgotten the ancient ceremonies of symbolic marriage that once took place both in the spring and again at Midsummer.

In Sweden the Midsummer Bride chose herself a mock bridegroom, and members of the community took up a collection for the pair, who were looked upon as man and wife. Youths in the village were free at this time also to choose a temporary bride.

In the Italian island of Sardinia, these summer Solstice couples were known as the Sweethearts of St. John, and their celebrations featured pots of sprouting grain—as if to emphasize the connection between human sexuality and the fertility of nature. The rite began in March, when a young man of the village might present himself to a girl, requesting that she be his *comare* (sweetheart), and offer to be her *compare*. This invitation was nearly always accepted. Some weeks later, the girl made a pot out of cork, filled it with soil, and planted wheat and barley seeds in it. By Midsummer, the plants had matured enough to have formed heads of grain. Then the couple, dressed in their finest and accompanied by a parade of adults and children, walked to the church at the edge of the village, where they broke the pot against the church door. All sat in a circle on the grass and shared a picnic of eggs and herbs and passed a cup of wine. Then they joined hands and sang "Sweethearts of St. John" (*Compare e comare di San Giovanni*) again and again to the accompaniment of flutes. At last they stood and danced in circles until evening.

Frazer notes that when our ancestors staged such picturesque rites

> they were doing something far more important than merely putting on a pastoral play for the amusement of a rustic audience. They were performing a serious magical rite, designed to make the woods grow green, the fresh grass sprout, the corn shoot, and the flowers blow. . . . Accordingly we may assume with a high degree of probability that the profligacy which notoriously attended these ceremonies was at one time not an accidental excess but an essential

part of the rites, and that in the opinion of those who performed them the marriage of trees and plants could not be fertile without the real union of the human sexes.[12]

This was about as close as the Victorian Frazer was likely to get to a discussion of the energetic dynamics of sacred sexuality, a subject that has been treated with intelligence and vision in more recent times by Dolores LaChapelle and Georg Feuerstein.[13] The Chinese Taoists and the Tantric yogins of India saw ritualized sexuality as a way of increasing the life essence and of promoting spiritual enlightenment through the movement of subtle energies up the spine. Lachapelle writes:

> Ritualized sex in both primitive societies and in Taoism comes out of entirely different roots than sexual activites in Western culture, where the emphasis has always been on procreation. In the latter culture, male ejaculation is of great importance because it is tied in with fertility and the male ego. In ritualized sex, however, the main concern is "dual cultivation" and bonding within the group and with nature.[14]

The ancients believed that when a woman and man become energetically balanced and attuned through prolonged, ecstatic intercourse, they transmit a harmonizing influence throughout society and nature. And they believed that such harmonizing influences were particularly needed—and effective—at the times when Heaven and Earth are at their extremes—i.e., the Solstices.

Burying the Carnival:
the Mock Funerals of Midsummer

In Tsarist Russia, Midsummer was marked by the fashioning of an effigy in straw of a being called Kupalo or Kostroma. The people dressed this straw man in women's clothes and adorned it with a necklace and a crown of flowers. Then a tree was cut, decked with ribbons, and set up on a propitious spot. This tree was given the name of Marena (winter, death), and near it was placed the straw figure and a table with food and drink. Then a bonfire was prepared, over which young men and women would jump, holding Kupalo in their arms. On the following day the straw figure and the tree were both stripped and thrown into a stream.

In the Murom district the assembled crowd divided itself into two groups, which fought over the effigy, one attacking it and the other defending. Eventually the hostile group would win, tearing the straw figure to bits while the defenders pretended to bewail and mourn the death of Kostroma. In Little Russia a similar tradition surrounded a figure known as Yarilo, which was laid in a coffin and paraded through the streets and mourned loudly by the local women. And in Austria and Germany like customs prevailed, which were there known as "Burying the Carnival" or "Carrying Out Death."

The point of these rites, according to Frazer, was the celebration of the summer Solstice and the mourning of the Sun:

> . . . the decline of summer is dated from Midsummer Day, after which the days begin to shorten, and the sun sets out on his downward journey—"To the darksome hollows where the frosts of winter lie." Such a turning-point of the year, when vegetation might be thought to share the incipient though still almost imperceptible decay of summer, might well be chosen by primitive man as a fit moment for resorting to those magic rites by which he hopes to stay the decline, or at least to ensure the revival, of plant life.[15]

The ancients no doubt found meaning in the irony that at the peak of light and life, at the summer Solstice, there is the seed of death, darkness, and decay; while the reverse is true at Midwinter. And herein perhaps lies the motive that gave rise to the disparate motifs—of flowers, fires, weddings, and funerals—that accompanied the Midsummer festival: it was a celebration of transformation. Frazer suggested that " . . . the flowers, like the fires of midsummer, are thought to transfer to mankind some effulgence of the sun's light and heat which invests them for a time with powers above the ordinary for the healing of diseases and the unmasking and baffling of all the evil things that threaten the life of man."[16] At Midusmmer, in the blooming of a flower, in fire, in sex, and in death, energies are released, a moment of transformation arrives, and Heaven and Earth are for a moment reunited. And then, life goes on.

CHAPTER 9

The Meaning of the Solstices

THE SOLSTICES ARE INTRINSICALLY meaningful cosmic-terrestrial events, and at the same time powerful symbols for the deepest processes of transformation in the individual and collective human psyche.

At the heart of the ancient Solstice festivals was a profound regard for cycles. Every cycle—whether a day, a year, a human lifetime, or the life of a culture—has a beginning, a middle, and an end; and nearly every cycle is followed by another. Wisdom consists in knowing one's place in any given cycle, and what kinds of action (or restraint of action) are appropriate for that phase. What is constructive at one time may be destructive at another.

It was this kind of sensitivity to cycles of change that served as the basis for the ancient Chinese philosophy embodied in the *I Ching*, the Book of Changes. We read, for example, regarding the hexagram called *Fu* (The Return, or The Turning Point):

> The time of darkness is past. The winter solstice brings the victory of light. . . . After a time of decay comes the turning point. The powerful light that has banished returns.

There is movement, but it is not brought about by force . . . the movement is natural, arising spontaneously. For this reason the transformation of the old becomes easy. . . .

The idea of RETURN is based on the course of nature. The movement is cyclic, and the course completes itself. Therefore it is not necessary to hasten anything artificially. Everything comes of itself at the appointed time. This is the meaning of heaven and earth. . . .

The winter solstice has always been celebrated in China as the resting time of year. . . . In the winter the life energy . . . is still underground. Movement is just at its beginning; therefore it must be strengthened by rest, so that it will not be dissipated by being used prematurely. . . . The return of health after illness, the return of understanding after an estrangement: everything must be treated tenderly and with care at the beginning, so that the return may lead to a flowering.[1]

While some cycles are obvious—in human development, in the seasons, and in the motions of the Moon and Sun—others are subtle. Moreover, we tend to be aware of cycles to the degree to which we pay attention to them and move with them. As we have seen, ancient cultures *participated in* the seasonal cycles that shaped their daily lives and their yearly calendars. We in the modern industrial world have far more precise scientific knowledge of the motions of the planets and of biochemical cycles in plant, animal, and human physiology. And yet our knowledge is sterile. We observe the dance of life in rigorous detail, but we have forgotten how to move with the beat.

Ancient peoples believed that it is dangerous and foolish to ignore cycles. Perhaps we are discovering the truth of that bit of wisdom the hard way. In many areas of human affairs we have convinced ourselves that there should be only constant, unending growth. Our population can only increase. Our economies must expand. Civilization must spread. Technology must proliferate and complexify. In each case, we have decided that contraction would mean disaster. And yet further expansion and growth means disaster, too. Is it possible that our dilemma results partly from our ignorance of natural rhythms?

World Renewal

In even the most diverse cultures, the Solstice has been equated with the idea of world renewal—the understanding that at periodic intervals nature and human affairs reach a point of ending and of beginning again. The Solstice itself is such a time, but it is also a symbol of even greater turning points.

Communities, cultures, and civilizations germinate, blossom, and die. But this is a fact whose implications we often seem determined to ignore.

For centuries, religious prophets have been warning that the world is about to end. They were usually right. Many worlds have ended. The Middle Ages was a world that ended. Likewise Imperial China. Pre-Columbian America was a world our archaeologists are only beginning to appreciate; its ending was recorded by some of the people who helped bring it about. New worlds have begun, as well. One could cite the dawn of the industrial age, the colonial era, the electronic age, and so on, all within the past five centuries.

We today are living in a world that is in the process of dying and renewing itself. In our case, because we have achieved something like a global civilization, this death and this birth are on a scale that is difficult to comprehend. Nevertheless, from a sufficiently distant historical perspective, it may be possible to see this gargantuan, tempestuous transformation as the end of a grand cycle, perhaps composed of many smaller cycles all winding down at once; a cycle whose beginning reaches back many millennia to the origins of agriculture, centralized government, and organized religion.

The ancients, in their wisdom, believed that the principles at work in the births and deaths of world ages have their analogies in the beginnings and endings of much smaller cycles, such as the ones bounded by dawn and dusk, and the summer and winter Solstices. They would tell us that rejoicing and mourning are both necessary aspects of life. We may want youth to last forever, but it doesn't; and maturity and even death carry their own essential meanings.

When the time for disintegration and death comes, it is important to acknowledge the fact, to mourn, and to let go, so that there is clear space in which to welcome new life.

Our civilization has grown far in certain directions. Like a revered old general, we have many victories to recite: we have gained extraordinary control over nature; we have created awesome military power; we have developed an abstract and flexible market economy that is capable of producing and transferring wealth in quantities and at speeds that boggle the imagination. But there are natural limits to further conquests along these lines. The world in which these achievements made sense is coming to an end. If we are wise, we will acknowledge the fact and mourn, leaving space for something new.

These days, many people scoff at the term *New Age*, apparently because they believe that the present age will somehow continue indefinitely. How people who have grown up amid the furious and accelerating political, economic, social, and technological changes of the twentieth century could hold such a view is a matter for discussion elsewhere, possibly in the context of an exploration of the psychological phenomenon of denial. That there will be a New Age is beyond doubt—only its character is in question. As the ancients knew so well, the health of a nascent cycle is largely conditioned by the way in which the previous cycle was released: whether gently or violently; with compassion or animosity; with courage or fear.

Letting Go of the Past; Welcoming the New

The theoretical desirability and necessity of letting go of the past and welcoming the new is so obvious as to require little comment. We all know that the world is constantly changing and that we must adapt if we are to survive. We also know that change—in the forms of birth, death, the formation and dissolution of relationships, learning, aging, and so on—is inevitable in our personal lives, and that in most cases to resist such change is futile and foolish. In their festivals and rites of passage, ancient peoples *ritually* said goodbye to people, relationships, and experiences that were passing away, and opened themselves to receive whatever life now had in store.

By and large, we have lost these rituals, with the negligible exception of New Year's Day and its half-hearted resolutions, school graduations, and weddings. It might at first thought seem paradoxical, then, that it was the ancients, with their pervasive rites of change, who lived in stable societies with ordered and natural rhythms; while we, with few such rites, live in a whirlwind of social, economic, and technological metamorphosis.

Often change overwhelms us. For example, we tend to acquiesce without thought to the introduction of relatively untested technologies that alter the very fabric of our lives—from television to computers to nuclear energy to biological engineering. Theoretically, it should be possible for us to delay or control such far-reaching technological innovations—to subject them to scrutiny and agree together whether to go ahead with them, to wait until their side effects are better understood, or to reject them altogether. Yet we seldom exercise this theoretically possible control. We regard technological innovation almost as a force of nature; its implications for our children and our children's children are hardly even a matter for discussion. It is apparently impossible for us to "just say no" when it comes to technology.

Perhaps our fundamental cultural relationship with *change itself* has become dysfunctional. We have few social means for the expression of grief either for personal loss or for our collective losses—the loss of lands, lifestyles, and traditions that are disappearing wholesale with the onrushing technological and economic transformation of the planet. And just as we seem unable to give closure to the past, we seem equally unable to formulate any coherent vision of the future, and we often seem to lack both the courage and the imagination to initiate changes that are obviously needed in our personal lives and in our institutions—changes that would help end racism, violence, the abuse of nature, and extreme economic inequality.

It would be simplistic to suggest that the world's problems would be solved if only we all celebrated the Solstices together. But perhaps we could begin to refocus our attitudes toward change on these occasions, if we regarded them as opportunities to ritually release our grip on ideas and lifestyles that are clearly putting future generations at risk, and to commit ourselves to desperately needed personal and social action.

The Solstices of History

Our current global situation corresponds in some ways analogously both with the summer and with the winter Solstices. As at Midsummer, when the length of daylight finds its peak, our technological domination of nature and the sheer size of the global human population are near a peak. Present trends cannot continue much further (more than, say, another few decades). Both population densities and rates of resource depletion will decline in the next century, whether by deliberate plan or as the result of famine and environmental collapse.

Meanwhile, as at Midwinter, when the Sun is low in the sky, the innate life energies of the planet have been driven underground (figuratively, if not literally); and the spiritual light of the world's indigenous cultures is dim and close to the horizon of extinction.

Historically, it is at junctures like these that cultures undergo fundamental transformations. It is possible, for example, to draw many analogies between our civilization and that of Rome at the time of its fall. Like us, the Romans were facing crises of overpopulation and resource depletion; like us, they were saddled with an unresponsive governmental bureaucracy. The city's population approached one million at its height, a level that could be sustained only by extensive colonization, slavery, intensive farming, public works projects, and a welfare program. Virtually the entire known world was systematically pillaged in order to maintain the power and comfort of well-to-do Roman citizens. But the process could not continue indefinitely. Italy's agricultural system underwent progressive collapse, the military began to absorb more wealth than it could produce through further conquest, and Rome's bureaucracy ballooned to unmanageable proportions. During the four hundred years after the city's fall, its population plummeted to only about thirty thousand.

While the collapse of the Roman Empire produced widespread chaos and led to the so-called Dark Ages, people throughout Europe, northern Africa, and the Near East were freed from the yoke of imperialism; they consequently returned to a decentralized and, in many cases, more productive and stable mode of life. For centuries afterward, medieval towns were governed in a relatively democratic fashion by guilds of artisans and served as a bulwark against the centralist power struggles of the church and the nobility.

It is entirely likely that something like this will happen globally in the next few decades or centuries, though of course the enormous difference in scale between the Roman Empire and the industrial empires of the present will strain the analogy in many respects. In that event, it is possible that humanity could recover some of its former sense of the sacredness of nature, and that human cultures might regain some of their variety, vigor, and self-reliance. But it is also possible that the world could simply descend into chaos. Hence the importance of planting the seeds of sustainable culture now.

Acknowledging the Sources of Order and Light

The winter Solstice has always been a time to pray for the return of order and light, while the summer Solstice is an occasion to celebrate and give thanks for their abundance. But where do order and light come from? We have become accustomed to thinking that they derive from political and religious institutions, but our ancestors knew otherwise. They knew that we human beings exist in much larger ecological and cosmic systems and must abide by the rules of those systems if we are to survive. And the Solstices were ideal times to acknowledge and celebrate our responsibilities to these greater realms of Being.

True, we humans do create order in various forms, but on a limited scale. Our institutions may outlast individual human lifetimes, but they come and go nonetheless. Meanwhile, everything we do exists within another context, with its own inexorable pulsations. We cannot interfere with those rhythms with impunity; when we try to do so, we merely frustrate ourselves. On the other hand, when we honor the deep, abiding cycles of nature and cosmos, our lives are filled with light.

In human consciousness, light appears as inspiration, and it is inspiration that generates music, art, religion, dance, and culture itself. Inspiration cannot be summoned on demand, nor can it be suppressed indefinitely, nor forced fully to conform with prejudices and expectations. Inspiration goes where it wills; it has its own innate agenda. Each new generation has its light, its vision, which the previous generation often finds incomprehensible. Inspiration may shatter previous conventions. And yet this fresh light carries with it the seeds of new order.

Order and light naturally give birth to one another; in the present human world, however, they are often at odds. Our centralized, bureaucratized social order is commonly opposed by fiery radicals, whose flaming rhetoric often yields more heat than illumination. Our challenge, then, is to found a new social order based not in ideology but in respect for the context of which we are a part: an order that does not try to deny or frustrate the light of inspiration, but that allows it free play.

At the Solstices, we humble ourselves to the eternal truth that the real sources of order and light are the Earth and the Sun. We let the artificialities of human institutions subside in importance, and we abandon ourselves to play. We renew the life of our social order by periodically abolishing it and allowing it to be reborn from the womb of nature.

Children, Play, and the Solstices

Solstice celebrations have always included children as enthusiastic participants. This is due not only to children's natural embodiment of the essences of renewal and of light but also to their irrepressible spontaneity. For at their root, all festivals are really excuses to play.

To the sociologist, play is behavior that appears enjoyable but has no obvious survival value. But such a description gives little hint of its profound role as the fundamental activity of exploring, stretching, and transcending the boundaries between beings. The most basic of all borders is that between Self and Other, and our attitude toward this basic existential boundary determines the quality of our experience of life. Are we defensive, aggressive, fearful, or playful?

The young of all birds and mammals play. Play deprivation studies with monkeys, such as those by Harry Harlow and his students, have shown that play is essential for the development of basic social skills, sexual behavior, and parenting.[2] As one might expect, the most intelligent mammals are also usually the most playful.

Play therapist Fred Donaldson, in his book *Playing By Heart*, writes of his years of experience with bridging cultural and species differences—and gulfs in communication between children and adults brought about by Down's syndrome and autism—through physical, rough-and-tumble play. He has also helped thousands of adults reconnect with their own spontaneous and authentic selves by drawing them into direct, playful, touching encounters in play workshops he has conducted in many countries. He makes the point that play is not just utilitarian (merely a device for teaching children to be better adults), nor is it only a pleasant pastime for the young. Play is a window into the sacred, a way of transcending differences and an opportunity to express the ecstatic energies of life itself. The degree to which civilization has marginalized play is the degree to which it has denied and suppressed life.

In hunting-and-gathering cultures, children are treated indulgently and they play almost continually and without restraint. For a traditional Aboriginal Australian child, life is a constant round of self-directed exploration and imitation, filled with running, throwing, balancing, and swimming. Children are largely left to themselves and come to their parents or other adults for physical or emotional nourishment when needed. Though they receive a minimum of discipline from adults, they tend to be sociable, friendly, and generous with one another, and confident of themselves and of their ability to operate successfully within their environment.[3]

With technological progress, however, attitudes toward children and play change. Anthropologist Patricia Draper followed the

!Kung San Bushmen of southern Africa as their society came into increasing contact with civilization. As the people became more settled, kept goats, and hunted and gathered less, they began to demand more obedience from their children. Childhood gradually ceased to be a time of freedom and became instead more one of preparation for the harshness of disciplined adult life. Still, the !Kung San say of their more "advanced" animal-herding neighbors, who are less indulgent and more strict, "They don't like children."[4]

Children in agricultural, animal-herding, and industrial societies receive far more formal discipline than do those of the "primitive" hunter-gatherers. Regular corporal punishment (which is virtually unknown among the latter) becomes an accepted facet of childhood training. Consequently, play diminishes, and with it the social skills and self-esteem that only play can teach.

At the end of the civilizing process, we have succeeded in creating an adult world that is serious and calculating, in which time is money and play is a waste of time. We have formalized the learning process in bureaucratic schools, "learning factories" that routinize children's daytime activities, while much of their remaining attention is devoted to the hypnotic glare of television. The joy of free interaction with other children of varying ages in a complex natural environment has largely disappeared.

As a substitute for spontaneous play, we civilized adults have created *games*: competitive, serious contests with winners and losers. We teach these contest-games (in which, according to Donaldson, "every victory is someone's funeral") to our children, in an effort to prepare them for life in our highly competitive, stress-filled adult world. Having denied and suppressed our own and our children's innate playfulness, we have created a society in which low self-esteem and poor socialization generate increasing crime and an array of self-destructive addictive behaviors.

The Solstice festivals were intended partly as an antidote to these illnesses of civilization and as an invitation to return to play. By ritually abolishing laws and hierarchies and by indulging in singing and dancing with childlike abandon during their seasonal celebrations, ancient peoples kept the formalities of adult life in perspective. No matter how earnestly they pursued their political and economic goals during the rest of the year, come festival time rich and poor alike returned (temporarily, at least) to the free, equal, anarchic status of the First People of the mythic Golden Age.

Sexuality and the Seasonal Festivals

The freedom and playfulness that characterized the Solstice festivals often found expression in orgiastic or ritual sex. This sanctioned and coordinated release of procreative energy served two important functions: it strengthened the bonds within the community, and served to stimulate and revitalize the land.

As Dolores LaChapelle notes in her book *Sacred Land, Sacred Sex: The Rapture of the Deep*, "World Renewal Festivals always include human sexual rites: the renewal of life cannot occur without sexual contact."

> In most traditional cultures human sexual activity was part of the on-going whole of all of life in that particular place. It had specific effects on the whole: positive when it contributed to the overall fertility of life as humans added their sexual activity to the ritual "increase ceremonies" of animal or plant life in that place and negative, when humans failed to keep the number of children within the limits of what that place could feed without damage. In the latter case, naturally, humans destroyed the basis of their own on-going life. Few traditional cultures did this for very long. They either died out or moved elsewhere or learned the rituals to enable them to stay. This is the basis of "sacred sex."[5]

In Europe, until fairly recent times, it was customary for rural couples to make love in their fields around the times of Beltane and Midsummer in order to ensure a bountiful harvest. This was a survival of much older fertility rites in which whole communities participated. But, as Mircea Eliade once wrote,

> . . . we must beware of misinterpreting these licentious excesses, for what is in question here is not sexual freedom, in the modern, desacralized sense of the term. In premodern

societies, sexuality, like all the other functions of life, is fraught with sacredness. It is a way of participating in the fundamental mystery of life and fertility.[6]

LaChapelle writes that "there's no sacred sex without sacred land."[7] As anyone who has spent much time in the wilderness will attest, nature is sexy. When the forces of life are coursing through trees and flowers and animals, similar currents tend to flow in us as well. Ancient peoples believed that the process was reciprocal: just as a beautiful spring day can arouse our amorous feelings, they believed that by the free expression of those feelings we evoke more of the same in nature. They saw life and sexuality as good and sacred, and so their rituals and festivals were occasions not for pious sanctimony but for ecstatic self-expression.

Our modern, Western industrial civilization retains only the merest vestiges of these ancient rites in the forms of mistletoe kissing and New Year's Eve dances. For us, sex has become an object, a problem—something profane and private, always to be practiced indoors. We seldom think of sex as sacred; it is never public or communal, except in a voyeuristic or pornographic sense; and it is hardly ever enjoyed outdoors, so we give no thought to its possible effects on the land. In our crowded, impersonal cities, intimacy carries so many risks of abuse and disease that it inspires more feelings of fear and dread than of celebration, playfulness, joy, or worship. How different was the experience of tribal peoples, like the Aboriginals of Australia. Robert Lawlor, in *Voices of the First Day*, writes that

> Aboriginal ritual sexuality, whose dynamism is so boundless that it excites and vitalizes all of nature, is based on a love for the earth and earthly life. It is not a love instigated by exploitative desire, conservationist zeal, or environmental piety. It is a love for the earth that expands from sexual passion. . . .[8]

Perhaps the recovery of seasonal festivals offers an avenue for the return of the joy and sacredness to sexuality. For the time being, full genital sex carries so much cultural baggage that it is nearly impossible to ritualize it publicly without invoking abuse and censure. Nevertheless, if such is the intent of the participants, it is unquestionably possible to promote a healthy expression of sexuality in the context of a modern Solstice celebration by way of dance, play, and humor. But this requires that, for the duration of the festival, those concerned give themselves as fully as possible to the collective drama without taking their feelings personally. In other words, each man must willingly set aside his own persona (as much as possible) and become an embodiment of the divine masculine; and each woman, an embodiment of the divine or archetypal feminine.

The Solstices as Celebrations of the Divine Feminine and Masculine

Every ancient culture had a creation story that told how the world began. But this story was not only an account of what happened in the distant past; it was also a description of the way creation occurs in the eternal present. Often the creation story told how the One, the universal primordial Being, split into two cosmic principles—masculine and feminine, Heaven and Earth—which then made love and gave birth to the Universe. In most ancient cultures, the sky was regarded as masculine, the Earth as feminine. Sunlight, lightning, and rain were seen to come down from the celestial Father to fertilize the the body of the Mother (our word *matter* comes from the Latin *mater*, meaning "mother"), which in turn gave birth to life in all its various forms.

As times when the cycles of Earth and sky reach their extremes, the Solstices were occasions that brought the divine masculine and feminine principles to ritual focus. The ancient Chinese, for example, believed that at sunrise on the winter Solstice the *yang* (masculine) principle was born into the world and commenced six months of ascendancy. It is more than coincidental that Christians celebrate the birth of a divine male child at the same time of year.

Again according to ancient Chinese Taoist traditions, the most propitious time to worship the Earth goddess is in the early morning on the summer Solstice. This is because "at this time the *yin* (female) principle is born and begins to wax strong. The *yang* principle begins to wane in power."[9] That there is no corresponding Midsummer Christian festival of the divine feminine is, perhaps, an indication of the degree of imbalance between cosmic-sexual principles in our civilization.

All cultures agreed that the first era of the world was a Golden Age of harmony when women and men, humanity and nature, and Heaven and Earth were united in loving understanding. But that time of harmony came to a tragic end, and ever since then division and strife have plagued us. For ancients, the Solstices were times to celebrate the polarities, to bring them into healthy relation, and thereby to recapture some of the harmony and joy of the Golden Age. We, having discarded these occasions for world rebalance and renewal, see consequences in the form of abusive, broken relations between women and men, between cultures, and between humanity and nature.

The solution to these imbalances and misunderstandings must come individually as well as collectively. Each of us must discover and nurture a sense of self-worth that comes from the core of our being, rather than from our physical appearance or worldly success. From that base of inner security we must learn to speak honestly about our needs and fears, our visions and dreams, without blaming others for our own feelings or expecting them to change to suit us.

When a man ignores and denies his feminine side, or a woman denies her masculine side, then each tends to *project* those undeveloped qualities onto others. For example, a man might see an attractive woman as the embodiment of everything he wants and needs; he will "fall in love," feeling that he can't live without her. But he is only seeing the projected image of his own needs; he cannot see the woman for who she really is. Or a woman may project the negative aspect of her undeveloped masculine side onto a man and find herself hating him—when what she really hates is the rejected part of herself. By coming to understand and accept ourselves, we also open the possibility of coming to understand others for who they really are.

The same principle holds true for cultures, and for humanity as a whole in its relations with nature. We will stop destroying

Mother Earth only when we stop projecting onto her the longings and fears we feel toward the denied or repressed feminine aspects of ourselves and our culture.

The recovery of the seasonal festivals could play a significant role in assisting the healing and reconciliation of the divine feminine and masculine in human society. As Dolores LaChapelle has written, "The great seasonal festivals, as done in traditional primitive cultures...balance[d] out the male and female in each person."[10] In the festival, the masculine and feminine divine essences were worshiped, embodied, and reconciled. And this was perhaps the greatest reason for these celebrations' effectiveness in maintaining the stability and vitality of the communities who held them.

For us in the modern world, perhaps the first priority in cultural renewal should be the revival of the Midsummer festival of the divine feminine. It is the true and natural Earth Day, a time when we can focus our attention on healing the denied and abused aspects of ourselves and the world, and on celebrating the nurturing, intuitive, ecstatic powers of archetypal woman.

On the Recovery of Culture

In the context of our modern industrial civilization, the discussion of Solstice celebrations seems perhaps interesting from an antiquarian perspective, but otherwise inconsequential. When we adopt a broader historical and cross-cultural vantage point, however, it is industrial civilization itself that appears strangely out of step.

Obviously, we have gained a great deal through the progress of the past few centuries. Our scientific knowledge of ourselves and of our world has expanded vastly, and a small portion of the human population now enjoys unprecedented power and wealth. But we have lost much, too.

For the ancients, the sky was a constant source of awe. One could hardly escape it. The constellations and planets, the phases of the Moon, the position of the Sun, all were noted throughout the day and much of the night by virtually everyone. Now we insulate ourselves from the lights in the sky. On a clear night (that is, when the smog isn't too thick or the city lights too bright), the typical modern has a hard time picking out more than one or two constellations and perhaps a single planet. The position of the Sun and the phases of the Moon are of little or no concern.

The same with our planetary home. Once, we saw the Earth as sacred and alive. The animals and plants were intelligent beings, our intimate companions whose songs and habits were woven into the fabric of our lives. Now we tend to think of the Earth as the sum of our economic resources, or as a political map.

We who have grown up in industrial civilization are accustomed to regarding it as the inevitable product of cultural evolution. We see factories, highways, and cities as natural and ordinary. Why not? This is all we have known. It is so easy to forget that civilization itself is a recent, unusual, and unstable development—in the history of our species. Yes, we have grown during these past decades and centuries, but we have grown so fast in one direction that we have become lopsided. And so our very survival may depend on our ability to grow in unaccustomed ways, to recover some of what we have lost, and thereby to rebalance ourselves.

As has happened so many times in human history, we may find that our next step forward will be inspired by a deepened appreciation of the past. Of course, we we are not prepared, as a society, to go back to ancient patterns of life in any literal sense. What is gone is gone, and there is wisdom in making use of what we have learned over the past centuries, rather than in repudiating those experiences and discoveries. But at the same time, we might acknowledge that in many respects we have gone off course. Cultural renewal means not a slavish imitation of archaic practices, but a change of direction back toward sustainability, decentralization, freedom, and responsibility. If some ancient cultural forms do seem worth reviving, we can be sure that they will be changed simply by the new consciousness we bring to them.

In many ways the Solstice festivals serve to symbolize the essence of what we have traded for civilization's advantages—our formerly intimate relationship with nature and cosmos. And so they may serve as ideal starting points for the recovery of culture.

In this book, I am suggesting that we bring our modern sensibilities to bear on the creation of *new* festivals that honor the intrinsic meanings of the Solstices in ways that are relevant for ourselves and our world. As scientifically educated people, we know that the Solstice isn't part of a cosmic ball game, as the Chumash envisioned it; we know that the seasons will continue to follow one another in an orderly rhythm even if we fail to build bonfires at the appropriate moment. Yet we still have an innate need to celebrate. We need occasions to come together, and we need to feel a part of something larger than ourselves and our families, something more intrinsically meaningful than our nations and corporations. As nearly all cultures have known for thousands of years, the celebration of the Solstices is the ideal way to fill all of these needs.

PART THREE

Festivals for Our Time

The last three thousand years of mankind have been an excursion into ideals, bodilessness, and tragedy and now the excursion is over...it is a question, practically, of relationship. We must get back into relationship, vivid and nourishing relationship to the cosmos. ... The way is through daily ritual, and the reawakening. We must once more practice the ritual of dawn and noon and sunset, the ritual of kindling fire and pouring water, the ritual of the first breath, and the last. ... We must return to the way of 'knowing in terms of togetherness'...the togetherness of the body, the sex, the emotions, the passions, with the earth and sun and stars.

—D. H. Lawrence

CHAPTER **10**

Celebrating the Solstices
On Your Own

I F YOU ARE OBSERVING THE SOLSTICE
by yourself or with a friend, you might want to take advantage of
some of the suggestions in this chapter; if you wish to assemble
a larger group for a festival, Chapter 11 offers ideas you might
find helpful. You may find some of the activities described in
this chapter personally useful *in addition to* events planned for a
larger gathering. Remember: these suggestions are only intended
to stimulate your own creative thinking. Unless you belong to a
living spiritual tradition with ongoing yearly Solstice rites, you will
need to use your imagination and inner sensing to find a way of
celebrating that is right for you.

Visit a Sacred Site

The landscape of every inhabited continent is dotted with
places of extraordinary meaning to indigenous peoples. In the earliest times these places were marked simply by the natural features of
the land—hills, trees, streams, springs, outcroppings of rock, caves,
or mountains. For Aboriginal Australians, Uluru (Ayer's Rock) is
still the ceremonial and mythological center of the continent; for

the Navajo, the sacred mountains of the four cardinal directions—conspicuous peaks surrounding the Four Corners region, where Colorado, New Mexico, Arizona, and Utah meet—have embodied the spirit of the Creators since the beginning of the present world.

Early agricultural peoples marked sacred sites with temples, standing stones, mounds, barrows, and other humanly-made structures. Such structures—including Stonehenge, the medieval cathedrals of Europe, Chaco Canyon in America, etc.—seem to have been built at natural sites already hallowed by long tradition.

Why were these places set apart? In some instances, where there are unusual or majestic land features that spontaneously inspire feelings of awe and transcendence, the answer would appear obvious. But some sacred sites seem at first to be quite ordinary. According to the traditions of indigenous peoples, the sacredness of a site has little to do with our ideas about breathtaking natural scenery; a place is sacred because it carries a certain energy or spirit.

Virtually all archaic peoples believed in the existence of an energy that pervades and vivifies the landscape. Certain places have differing quantities or qualities of this energy. The Chinese Taoists spoke of it as *qi* (or *chi*). It is a power also present in the human body and throughout the Universe. The vitality of the land, and therefore of the people, depended upon the proper balance and flow of living *qi* as it passed through streams, valleys, and hills. The Chinese sages created *feng shui* to mediate the Earth currents and to identify suitable places for homes, temples, and graves.

The Dragon Project of Cornwall, England, headed by author Paul Devereux (*Places of Power*), has explored ancient stone circles, standing stones, barrows, etc., with magnetometers, Geiger counters, voltmeters, and ultrasound sensors, and has documented anomalous magnetic fields, ultrasound emissions, and radiation patterns at many of these sites.

In *The New View Over Atlantis*, John Michell, one of the modern pioneers in the rediscovery of the original purpose of ancient sacred places, writes:

> Like all other heavenly bodies, the earth is a great magnet, the strength and direction of its currents influenced by

many factors including the proximity and relative positions of the other spheres in the solar system, chiefly the sun and moon. Other influences on the strength and activity of the magnetic current derive from the composition of the ground over which it passes. Over firm, flat country it is placid and regular, while over rocky, broken land it becomes violent and disturbed, reacting with the elements to cause magnetic storms and, in northern regions, auroras and polar lights. In the neighbourhood of geological faults the magnetic flow becomes particularly agitated due to the springs of current which at these places burst through the earth's crust.[1]

Modern science is gradually coming to realize that the human body is sensitive to minute variations in electromagnetic fields. Robert O. Becker, M.D., a principal researcher in the field of bioelectricity, has discovered that EM fields can either positively or negatively influence limb regeneration, the development of cancers and other illnesses, as well as our general state of consciousness. Much of Becker's work has centered on the demonstration of the harmful effects of the powerful, artificial fields produced by power lines, house wiring, etc. At the same time, in his book *The Body Electric*, he suggests that our deepening understanding of the bioelectricity of growth will someday revolutionize our ability to heal injuries and illnesses of many kinds.

The Earth's natural magnetism has a twenty-seven-day cycle of quiet and disturbance. It varies also with respect to the seasons, and over vastly longer intervals of thousands and millions of years. It seems that ancient peoples not only were aware of this magnetic current (which is still apparent to anyone with a knack for dowsing), but attuned the rhythms of their communities to it. Their sacred sites were intuitively chosen as places where the energies of the cosmos, of the Earth, and of the human organism could harmonize.

Dowsers say that most ancient sacred sites still exude subtle energies, and increasing numbers of people are undertaking pilgrimages to Uluru, Chaco Canyon, Avebury, Glastonbury Tor, and so on, in order to experience these energies for themselves. Many who spend time at these places report being changed by the experience. Some say that sites where the ancients held festivals and ceremonies at the Solstices and Equinoxes seem especially charged at those times of the year.

You needn't undertake an expensive journey to one of these famous spiritual centers in order to experience the sacredness and power of place. There are probably geocosmically special sites in your area, where you may not only recharge your own spiritual batteries but (more importantly) help in the resanctification of the land. Use your intuition; ask around. Walk the land with an open heart and a clear mind. Explore nearby county, state, and national parks and wilderness areas. Notice the line of the horizon, the quality of light, and the activities of birds and other animals. The actual geographic features present—whether hills, a lake, a stream, a valley, or a plain—are of course significant in their contribution to the *feeling* of the place. But pay attention as well to your inner landscape: as you're walking, notice when your mind clears or your body feels light and relaxed. Certain places may elicit mental imagery, perhaps in the form of memories of moments from your childhood.

Once you have found a place that feels special to you, ask the spirit of that place for permission to be there. If you have little feeling of respect for the land, you are not likely to have much of an experience of its sacredness.

Spend all or part of the Solstice at the sacred place you have found, alone or with friends. While you are there, meditate not only on receiving healing and insight, but also on ways you can offer more care, reverence, and protection for the Earth and her creatures.

Connect More Deeply with the Land Where You Live

One of the benefits of finding your own local sacred site (as opposed to buying a plane ticket to London and then hopping a bus to Stonehenge) is that doing so helps you to feel a deeper connection with the land in the area where you live.

Particularly in North America, the vast majority of people are either immigrants, or descendants of immigrants (or of people who were kidnapped, sold, and brought here against their will). Most of us live in cities, many of us in apartments or condominiums. When we travel, we see the same stores in the shopping malls and the same fast-food restaurants on street corners wherever we go. Increasingly, every place tends to look like every other place, and, as we move from city to city, we take little notice of the subtle differences in soil, rocks, trees, birds, and weather. As our environments become as interchangeable and replaceable as parts on an assembly line, we ourselves—insulated by our cocoonlike lifestyles from any possibility of engagement with, or commitment to, the land—gradually tend to lose our individuality and character as well.

Indigenous peoples such as the Aboriginal Australians felt a responsibility to *look after* the land. This implied not only a detailed practical knowledge of topography and ecology, but a lifelong development of skill in observing and communicating with animals, harvesting wild plants at the right times and in properly restricted quantities, and setting fires at the appropriate times and places so as to "clean" the land and allow for new germination and growth. For peoples such as these, world renewal was not merely a spiritualized hope or longing, but a practical daily pursuit.

As mere consumers, we have lost our sense of responsibility—which, after all, is the *ability to respond*: the ability to sense and align with the fundamental rhythms of nature and of life itself as it bubbles up from the core of our being. To regain our proper human responsibilities, we must begin to take more of an interest in the welfare of our immediate natural surroundings.

As a way of preparing for the Solstice, check your library for books on native flora and fauna. Each place has its unique climate, plants, animals, rocks, feel, and spirit. Learn the names of the herbs, flowers, birds, mammals, and insects in your area. Spend time outdoors simply being quiet and paying attention.

Learn the boundaries of your *bioregion*—which has been defined as any distinct place with a continuity of watersheds, rivers, landforms, climate, native plants and animals, and human settlements and cultures shaped by these characteristics, and that has in the past, at least by some people, been defined as a home place.

You might wish to learn more about *bioregionalism*—a practical political and economic philosophy of which two principal exponents are Stephanie Mills and Peter Berg. Essentially, bioregionalism is about asking oneself the question "Where?" Where am I going to stay? Where will I declare my loyalty? Where will I exercise citizenship? Where is the place I belong? Bioregionalists are local caretakers who take the time and trouble to know and responsibly use the natural resources of their local environment, and to actively participate in the decision making processes of their local community.

As a way of marking the Solstice, determine the boundaries of your bioregion and make a bioregional map, showing watersheds, streams, and other major land features. Do some more research and find out: What are the public issues for this region? What are the proposed development projects, dams, highways, etc., in your area, and what are their potential effects? Are there local groups already working to "look after the land"? What can you do to help? Once you know *where* you are, and feel committed to being there, you will find yourself participating far more naturally and deeply in Earth's seasonal round. The Solstices, after all, are not merely abstract astronomical phenomena, but local occasions for the evocation and sharing of basic feelings of interdependence and connectedness.

Observe a Wild Animal

My partner Janet and I live in a little house in rural Sonoma county. Last spring a pair of house finches built a nest on our front porch, just outside our kitchen windows. Every time we entered the kitchen we looked to see how the bird family was doing. Mamma bird sat on the nest, leaving for only a few minutes a couple of times a day. Papa bird showed up every hour or so to sing to her and to feed her.

House finches aren't unusual birds, and it is common for them to build nests on porches. The whole incident hardly seems worth relating, but for the effect of the birds' presence on our lives. It took me a few days to notice: every time Janet and I stopped to commune with the bird family, our stress levels plummeted. During these weeks Janet was adjusting to a new office job, and I was having trouble finding editorial work. There were days when our nerves were raw. But whenever our attention was drawn to the finches, we found our voices growing quieter and sweeter, our breathing deepening, our shoulders relaxing.

The thought occurred to me: with taxes, commuter traffic, credit card debt, and the general pace of life in modern industrial civilization, few people can escape the harmful effects of stress. Many pay large sums of money to find ways to relax. The finches outside our window were giving us quite a benefit. All we could offer in return was to put up a little bird bath two yards from the nest. I set out some millet, but neither pappa nor mamma bird was interested. They were comfortable with us, but not dependent on us. We got some bird books from the library and read first about house finches, and then about other local birds.

Since then I've practiced hearing individual bird voices. Before, when I wasn't paying attention, I found that bird calls all tended to blend together; the experience was rather like being on a crowded street in a country whose language I couldn't understand. But as I began to listen, I realized that each bird species has a unique personality, and that each individual bird voices its interests and concerns, just as we do. Gradually, my bird-listening came more to resemble the experience of eavesdropping on animated and interesting conversations at a café.

The best way to observe wild animals is of course to spend time outdoors. As preparation, read Tom Brown's *Field Guide to Nature Observation and Tracking*. The Solstices and Equinoxes are ideal times to spend a day watching the wildlife in your local state park or nature preserve. Find a good place to sit and be for a couple of hours. Of course, you'll see somewhat different animals at different times of the year. Bring as few expectations as possible. Simply be fully *present* (and quiet), observing closely without *trying* to communicate with the animals you see. Don't try to analyze or name them; just let go of your sense of time and watch.

Become an Ecological Activist; Get Involved!

The Solstices are the original Earth Days. On these occasions, ancient peoples thought about world renewal in terms consistent with their cultures. Rather than seeking to recreate their ceremonies, we might ask ourselves, *What are the practical channels for world renewal in our time?* For me, the answer to that question has much to do with environmental activism.

These days we are beginning to realize that we have put far too much value in technology and possessions and far too little in nature. We have treated nature as a means, when it is an end in itself—our ultimate model and standard for what is *good*. We have prized everything new and artificial and have taken the land, trees, water, herbs, and animals for granted. It's time to change.

Some people have made protecting and restoring the Earth their mission in life; not all of us can do that. Hopefully, we are contributing to the world in other ways. Nevertheless, those who are on the vanguard need our support.

Find out who is doing the work that you think is important—locally as well as nationally or internationally. What cause moves you—Animal rights? Conservation? Human rights? Agricultural reform? The preservation of indigenous cultures? Ask yourself: What will help our society become more responsible, sane, and humane? And then: how can I help?

Talk is cheap; actions matter. As North Americans, we are responsible for much of the world's pollution, resource depletion, and environmental degradation. This doesn't mean that we should feel guilty for having been born into this culture of plenty. It does mean that, as we awaken to the global situation and our role in it, we have a responsibility to do something.

Of course, we can engage in activism any day—we needn't wait for the Solstice. But on a day set aside to honor the Earth and her rhythms, it is natural to want to act on our concerns. The Solstice is an excellent occasion to make a commitment, to make specific plans, and to write a check to an organization that is making a difference.

If you don't already know, find out where recycling areas are in your town. Make an inventory of your lifestyle. What can you do without? Twenty years ago, the visionary economist E. F. Schumacher wrote that wisdom lies in simplifying and reducing our needs, not in expanding them endlessly. Is the purpose of life merely to accumulate as many consumer products as possible? If not, then the less time we devote to gadgets and waste, the more we will have to devote to what is intrinsically meaningful in life.

Plant a Tree

As we have seen, the ancients regarded trees as sacred and gave particular attention to them at the Solstices. These days, the world's old-growth forests are disappearing rapidly, with dire effects for wildlife and (eventually) for ourselves as well. Trees, after all, are the lungs of the planet. Each year a total area of forest the size of England disappears in order to satisfy our demand for paper, furniture, building materials, and packaging.

Conservation and reforestation efforts are obviously essential. But differing motives for such efforts will produce clearly differing results. If our concern is merely to ensure that we will continue to have adequate supplies of timber resources, then our solution will likely be to genetically engineer fast-growing trees, and to plant them in straight rows on carefully planned and tended tree farms. If, however, we are motivated by a reawakened sense of the sacredness and *inherent* value of other life forms, then we will tend to cherish and protect the remaining "wild" forest ecosystems and to reintroduce indigenous tree species wherever possible. The difference between the two approaches amounts to a fundamental choice between a world that is entirely engineered according to present human desires, or one that still offers humankind the archetypal encounter with the Other—a natural world we cannot fully understand or control, but from which we can learn and with which we can play.

If the second motive is to prevail, then we must begin now individually to form and renew our sacred bonds not so much with nature in general, as with nature in the particular—that is, with individual places, trees, land features, animals, etc. An excellent place to start is with a tree on your land or in your apartment.

This winter Solstice, instead of putting a dead tree in your living room, plant a live one in the ground. Ideal planting and transplanting times vary from species to species and from one climate zone to another, but in general, it's best to transplant balled and burlapped saplings in cool weather when they are dormant. Therefore winter Solstice may be a propitious time from the tree's standpoint, if the ground is soft enough. It may also be a good time to do some pruning of dead, diseased, or crossed branches on existing trees.

Find some good books on tree care in your library (excellent ones to look for are *The Simple Act of Planting a Tree*, by Tree People, with Andy and Katie Lipkis, and *The Earth Manual*, by Malcolm Margolin) and learn how to look after your trees. Note the guidelines for planting and also for pruning: prune only when necessary (to remove dead, diseased, or crossing branches), and if you're pruning limbs make your final cut close to but not flush with the trunk; that way, the wound will gradually heal over. Never top your trees or prune in the middle of a branch, as such cuts cannot heal and will encourage disease.

When you are choosing your Solstice tree, pick one that will thrive in your area (for example, if you live in southern California, investigate drought-tolerant varieties). What species are indigenous to your region?

Make a commitment to the welfare of the trees on your property or in the neighborhood where you live. Locate any nearby old-growth forest. Is it threatened? What can you do to help protect it?

Go On an Energy Fast

On a recent winter Solstice my partner and I decided to stay home and to use no electric lights or appliances for twenty-four hours so that we could participate more directly in the Earth's rhythm of light and dark. On the afternoon of December twentieth we hid all our clocks, unplugged the phone, ate dinner by candlelight, and retired early, awakening naturally just before sunrise on the morning of the Solstice. That day we felt more fully alive than usual, more relaxed, more attentive, and—I can find no more accurate word—*happier*.

Of course, untold millions of people lived without electricity day in and day out until the twentieth century, and hundreds of millions in the Third World still do, and their experience is certainly not one of uniform happiness. But for most modern urban Americans, the experience of a day without artificial light and electrical appliances is unusual, unsettling, and (it seems to me) highly therapeutic.

When energy is available literally at our fingertips, awaiting only the flick of a switch, it is easy to take it for granted. In most cases, our only participation in the process by which that energy is produced and distributed is the act of writing a check to the utility company. When we use energy so unthinkingly we tend to become addicts. We feel helpless without our "drug," and so we unconsciously assume that any threat to its supply would be a threat to our very existence. If told that the production of our drug involves the ecological equivalents of slavery, stealing, or murder, we try to ignore the news so as not to have to face the intolerable double bind.

The only way to free ourselves from this bondage to unconscious consumption is to take deliberate action—if not to go "cold turkey," then at least to make our use of energy a conscious choice rather than a reflex. Tackling an addiction may be hard work, but there are always rewards. The act of facing one's energy dependency tends to yield a new sense of self-reliance as well as feelings of connectedness with what lies outside the artificially structured reality that is daily reinforced by the various carrots and sticks of industrial civilization. An energy fast offers an opportunity to witness and participate in the ordinary miracles of day and night, of Sun and Moon, to a far greater depth than is usually the case. Each time I go on an energy fast, I find myself awed by the "ordinary" miracle of being alive on planet Earth, and am reminded that the things we tend to take for granted—air, water, light—are the most precious and beautiful gifts imaginable.

Make plans to spend the Solstice at home, consuming as little as possible of gasoline, electricity, and packaging. Take note of what you do use, and if you find that it satisfies a genuine need (as does food, for instance), then give it your full attention and enjoy it unreservedly. If you find yourself getting bored, examine your boredom; see where it comes from. Deliberately break habits; explore the limits of your creativity.

You may wish to extend your energy fast beyond twenty-four hours. One simple and rewarding way to do this is to unplug your television set for a pre-determined period, such as two weeks or a month. Another is to find out, from your utility company, the hours of "peak use" (usually late afternoon and early evening). When you use electricity during these hours the rates are much higher than at other times. If you schedule a partial energy fast into your daily routine, taking these hours of peak use into account, you'll find yourself saving money as well as increasing your awareness of your demands on the environment. The Solstices and Equinoxes can then serve as occasions to review and renew your plans and commitments regarding lifestyle and consumption.

Watch Sunrise and Sunset

Sunrise and sunset are, in a sense, the daily equivalent of the Solstices. They are the natural boundaries of the day, just as the Solstices are boundaries of the year. They therefore represent ideal opportunities to reconnect with the biocosmic rhythms of nature.

The peoples of many ancient cultures honored sunrise and sunset as times of meditation, reflection, and renewal. The Hawaiian practice of *Ho'oponopono* consisted of evaluating the day and letting go of any enmities or other ill feelings while watching the Sun disappear below the horizon. At sunrise, the Navajo pray, "May I live well today!" The Vedic Aryans and ancient Egyptians greeted the Sun in the morning with ceremony and song.

Sunrise brings the opportunity of a new beginning, while sunset promises rest and the passage from orientation in the outer world of tasks and events to an internal focus on dreams and ideas—symbolized by the stars.

The ancients watched the horizon all year long, noting the sunrise and sunset points as they made their gradual journey north and then south again. It is at sunrise and sunset that we see the clearest evidence of the increments and stages of the year's passage.

When one lives away from cities, alarm clocks, and electric lights, it seems quite natural to get up just before sunrise. One can't help but notice that the Sun appears at a different spot on the horizon each day. By June, it rises considerably north of due East. At the latitude where I live, it comes up then at about 6 A.M. Daylight Time. It is a time of day well suited to meditation. From about 5 A.M. onward, you can feel the Earth gradually awaken. Birds stir as the sky grows light. Then, suddenly, the Sun is born from the northeast horizon and the air feels clean and charged.

As all photographers know, the light at sunset is magical. Colors are soft and golden; the world looks like a Maxfield Parrish painting.

I believe that it is essential to my own physical, mental, emotional, and spiritual health to periodically set aside concerns for what is to come or what has been and simply to acknowledge, give thanks for, and bless the day that is.

On the Solstices, get up in time to greet the Sun; then, later in the day, make it a point to stop what you're doing and pay attention to the sunset. If possible, find a place where your view to the horizon is unobstructed by buildings. This may require a short trip by bicycle, bus, or car. High ground is best. Spend at least a half hour gazing toward the west (avoiding staring directly at the Sun, of course). If you wear glasses, take them off: your eyes, nervous system, and pineal gland will all be nourished by the unrefracted sunlight. In the morning, say to yourself, as the Navajo do, "May I live well today!" In the evening, take your cue from the ancient Hawaiians and deliberately let go of any stress, discouragement, or anger you may have accumulated during the day. Salute the Sun and the Earth and the Life they embody—the Life that is so much greater than our individual human existences—and breathe deeply.

CHAPTER 11

Creating a Solstice Festival

AS WE'VE SEEN throughout this book, Solstice festivals have always served as ways for communities to renew themselves. These days, our communities are in dire need of renewal. By *community* I mean any gathering of people who live, work, worship, or play together. In gathering-and-hunting and simple horticultural societies, the band or village served the entire range of human communal needs at once. In industrial civilization, the various functions of community are fragmented into the institutions of family, school, corporation, church, service club, city, political party, and nation. Cities and nations have grown huge, impersonal, and hierarchical. Families often suffer from social traditions of gender and age dominance, giving rise to various dysfunctions. Churches often fritter away their potential for communal and individual empowerment in an ongoing, numbing process of theological indoctrination. Corporations are frequently run like fascist states, offering little opportunity for play or creativity. As a result of all these trends, many modern people enjoy only dribbles of nourishing communal experience in their lives.

Real community thrives on celebration and play. Therefore the revival of Solstice festivals, while certainly not offering a panacea for society's ills, could nevertheless help provide a basis for healing and reconnection in our collective affairs. The following suggestions are intended only as starting points for the design of your own unique, improvised festivals.

Find Your Circle

Who are the people that naturally compose your community? Who are the people with whom you naturally wish to celebrate? Think of your family, friends, neighbors, and co-workers. What bonds do you share? Don't exclude children.

Consider the organization of the event. Look at your Solstice gathering as a cocreation rather than as a lecture, or even as a party at which one person serves as host. Share the planning of the event with at least one other person.

Ancient peoples—particularly the gatherer-hunters—tended to be egalitarian and to conduct their collective affairs in circles, in which each person was autonomous and yet part of the larger whole; each participant was visible and accountable to every other. This, it seems, to me, is one of many ancient traditions modern people could profitably adopt and adapt. Hold your gathering in a circle. Even if a small group is leading the celebration, everyone present should feel as though she or he is contributing.

If you are celebrating with family, find activities that don't involve watching television. If it's the summer Solstice, go on a camping trip together. If it's the winter Solstice, find indoor activities that are fun but out of the ordinary. Whatever you choose to do, make sure that everyone is included and that their contribution is appreciated. See the suggestions regarding cooperative games later in this chapter.

If you plan to celebrate with co-workers, look for a non-office setting. Exclude alcohol from the festivities. Its presence will inevitably recreate the ambience of the typical office Christmas party. Find games or other ways of relating that break habitual structures of relationship, so that bosses, managers, and workers can simply be people together. Are there interpersonal tensions in the company? Is there a way to ease them playfully?

If you're celebrating with friends, find a way to initiate a discussion about your individual hopes, dreams, and fears. To the extent that friends feel safe to open up and speak frankly, discussions of this kind are nearly always profoundly nurturing for all concerned. Sometimes a ceremony can help create an atmosphere conducive to honest self-disclosure. You might suggest that each member of the circle bring a short prayer, poem, or song representing her dreams and visions for the next six months.

My partner and I often celebrate the Solstices, Equinoxes, and quarter days with friends. For example, we recently held a Samhain gathering in our home with fifteen friends from around the Bay area. This group had been meeting regularly once a month for over a year simply for the purpose of sharing one another's ideas, interests, experiences, and concerns. On this occasion, we sent invitations explaining just what Samhain is (see Chapter 2), and suggested that people call us so that we could coordinate food (the evening was to include a pot luck dinner). Since we were meeting on a Saturday, when none of us was working, we were able to spend most of the day together. We met at 2 P.M. and drove to a nearby state park and walked for an hour among the redwoods, then returned home and prepared and ate our meal. The evening began with a brief ceremony. Each person in the circle articulated a hope or prayer for the coming year. Then (as we do at all our meetings) we went around the circle again, each participant offering the essence of an idea or experience they'd like to discuss further with the group. We find when we do this that a consensus easily emerges as to what topics are "hot" and worth pursuing. For the next two hours we engaged in an open discussion based on those themes.

If you're creating a festival for neighbors, or for your service organization or church, give some thought to the question, How can a festival serve the interests of the people in this community? If the festival is to be open to everyone in town, look for co-sponsors. At the celebration, you might briefly mention issues in the community regarding land development, pollution, day care, aid for the homeless, etc.; you might also want to talk about local groups that are already involved in social action. But remember: your friends and neighbors are coming to have a good time, not to be harangued. In your invitations and flyers, and at the event itself, be sensitive to people's beliefs and boundaries ("Is this too weird? Is it New Age? Is it pagan?") and seek always to include rather than divide. Music, dance, and food are the essential ingredients in public celebrations.

I feel fortunate to live in an area where Solstice festivals are an accepted part of community life. For the past few years, authors Starhawk and Lusiah Teish have held winter Solstice festivals in the nearby town of Sebastopol at the local Community Center. Last year about three hundred locals turned out, many in imaginative costumes. The crowd was obviously in the mood to celebrate. The event had been advertised through flyers and by word of mouth. Starhawk initiated the evening with drumming; everyone joined in, using whatever was at hand as a percussion instrument. Then Starhawk and Teish spoke for a few minutes about their process of sensing the right focus for this year's ritual. They had arrived at the themes of change and new hope—both inspired by the collapse of the Soviet empire and by the results of the (then recent) '92 elections. Teish noted that, while they had prepared some possible group activities, "The spirit of the group tells us what to do." From then on we prayed, chanted, sang, drummed, and danced for nearly three hours in the cavernous, wood-floored community room. Our only source of light was a rotating, spotlit mirrored ball, whose cascading, ever-turning reflections made the room itself seem to spin like a galaxy. The evening ended with a long spiral dance, with everyone lustily chanting:

Rising, rising
The Earth is rising
Turning, turning
The tide is turning.

Whether your festival is for family, friends, co-workers, or neighbors, it can include a variety of elements and forms. The following are only a few of the many possibilities.

Play Cooperative Games

As we saw in Chapter 9, play is an essential aspect of all seasonal celebrations, and nothing will help the success of an event more than enjoyable group activities. Unfortunately, modern Westerners have come to associate play almost entirely with competitive games and sports. But, as Alfie Kohn notes in his book *No Contest: The Case Against Competition*, the struggle to overcome an opponent tends to take the fun out of sports and recreation.

> The constituents of enjoyment that are used to argue for recreational competition actually do not, for the most part, require competition at all. We do not need to try to beat other people in order to have a good time. Why then, are competitive games so popular? The first response is that the extent of their popularity may not be so great as we imagine, at least if participation is our standard of measure. Some people, of course, avoid or drop out of sports because of disabilities, other interests, an aversion to exercise, and so forth. But a huge proportion dislike such activities precisely because they are competitive.[1]

Kohn points out that competitive games make opponents out of friends. Even the most informal tennis match, for example, requires that the two players try to make each other fail. But there is an alternative—cooperative games, in which the players are partners rather than opponents.

As resources, look for Terry Orlick's books *The Cooperative Sports and Games Book* (1978) and *The Second Cooperative Sports and Games Book* (1982), as well as Jeffrey Sobel's *Everybody Wins: 393 Non-competitive Games for Young Children* (1983). As the authors suggest, sometimes a little creative thinking will yield a non-competitive alternative to a normally competitive game. Orlick offers the example of musical chairs, which in Kohn's words constitutes "a prototype of artificial scarcity." As normally played, the game eliminates one chair and one player per round. Orlick proposes instead that as each chair is removed, the players all try to find room on the chairs that remain. "In the end," writes Orlick, "all twenty children who started the game are delicately perched on one chair, as opposed to nineteen disappointed children standing on the sidelines with one 'winner' on one chair."[2]

For team activities, Sobel recommends "cooperative choosing":

> No one likes to be chosen last, but somebody has to be, right? Wrong! . . . Use birthdays, saying that everyone with a birthday in the first six months of the year is on one team, and the rest on the other. Or use the players' initials, with the first and last halves of the alphabet being the deciding factors.[3]

Sobel offers cooperative versions of jacks, pin the tail on the donkey, hot potato, hide and seek, jump rope, tag, basketball, billiards, and bowling; he also introduces dozens of entirely new games and activities for young children.

Orlick describes games that can be played by people of varying ages, from toddlers to adults. He also reports on cooperative games he has researched among non-Western cultures, from the Chinese to the Malay to the Inuit. He notes that organized, competitive games—particularly those promoted by professional sporting interests—are replacing traditional cooperative games in virtually all societies. "Before all traces of sharing and cooperative skills disappear," he urges, "we need to reassess their important place in our lives and our children's lives."[4]

Allan and Paulette MacFarlan's 1958 *Handbook of American Indian Games* (available in reprint from Dover) addresses this need. The authors note that "times and seasons were strictly observed for the playing of many [Indian] games."[5] Among the 150 games they describe, most requiring little or no equipment, is one called "Star Groups," in which each player is given sixteen pebbles of differing sizes. The "chief" (or leader) calls out the name of a constellation, and the players each try to make a diagram of that star group on the ground using their pebbles (big ones for bright stars, small ones for faint stars). Most modern non-Native players require star charts for reference. Other Indian games involve elements of chance (such as "Find the Chief"), guessing (such as "What do I hold"), or rough-and-tumble physical contact (as in "Bear Cave Chief").

If Orlick's, Sobel's, and the Macfarlans' books are hard to find at your local bookstores, try the public library.

Do Some Drumming; Sing and Dance

These days, in New Age circles as well as in many men's and women's groups, drumming is in vogue. For good reason. With recorded music so easily available, we have become a generation of music consumers rather than music makers. In primitive societies, everyone is a musician: from early childhood and throughout life, each person sings, dances, drums, and partakes of all the activities of a well-rounded life. But in our modern, civilized world nearly everyone is a specialist, and so it is usually only the most talented who have the courage and fortitude to learn to play an instrument. Only a tiny portion of the population has a chance to feel first-hand the exhilaration of playing in a good string quartet, orchestra, jazz combo, or rock band. The positive result of such specializa-tion is that we can vicariously delight in the wizardry of Itzakh Perlman playing Bach or Charlie Parker playing Cole Porter. But millions miss the simple joy of self-expression that music affords, because they believe they aren't talented enough to measure up to professional standards.

The solution, of course, is to simplify and democratize the musical experience so that more can participate. We needn't try to reduce Perlman or Parker to everyone else's level; but we also needn't compare ourselves with them to the extent that we inhibit ourselves from doing and playing what we can.

When we take music back to basics, we are left with our voices and our bodies—tone and rhythm. The very first sound that any of us heard—months before birth—was our mother's heartbeat. The second was her voice, its vibration conducted by bone and tissue.

In leading a Solstice festival, you may find that a drum, your own voice, and a candle are all the tools or props you need.

Buy or make a drum. Regard it as a sacred object. Get to know it by spending at least ten minutes a day drumming. Start with simple rhythms and learn to play evenly and steadily. Virtuosity is beside the point; continuity is everything. Learn to keep the same rhythm flowing for ten to twenty minutes. You'll find that doing so induces a light trance.

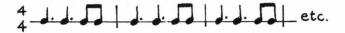

Listen to as many kinds and styles of drumming as you can— Native American, African, Latin American, Middle Eastern, East Indian, etc. An excellent resource is Mickey Hart's recording, *Planet Drum*, which is available at most record stores. You might also consult his book, *Drumming at the Edge of Magic*. Find a few (perhaps four) simple rhythms that you feel comfortable with, that *move* you, and master them.

Make a similar effort with song or chant: practice a few minutes a day, learning a few songs or chants by heart. Again, there is a vast cultural legacy to draw upon—European, Native American, African, etc. As a resource I recommend two tapes of chants and songs by Starhawk—*Let It Begin Now: Music from the Spiral Dance*, and *Chants: Ritual Music*.[6]

Learn a few folk dances as well—especially those performed in a circle. One dance that is particularly appropriate for larger Solstice gatherings is the spiral dance. The group begins in a circle, holding hands. The leader, playing a hand drum and singing, draws one end of the circle around and inward toward the center, in a gradual spiral.

The spiral dance

Upon reaching the center, the leader turns so that the spiral folds around on itself. As the line of dancers spirals, each dancer has the opportunity to face and greet (briefly) every other dancer. At last the line returns to a circle; or, the process can begin again.

Perform a Ceremony

Ceremonies or rituals are ideal for initiating or closing cycles. In essence, they are tools for focusing and changing consciousness.

A ritual can be sterile or hollow if it is performed without authentic emotional involvement. On the other hand, ceremonies that are powerfully emotional *can be* manipulative, and one could cite endless examples of the manipulative uses of ceremony from the religious and political history of the West, and from other cultures as well. Therefore it is important to use ceremony and ritual wisely, for purposes that are clearly understood from the outset by all involved. As a leader or participant, your object should not be to influence anyone else (either within or outside the group), but to provide a means of self-directed transformation for yourself and others.

Some ceremonies mark personal rites of passage—the beginning or end of a relationship, puberty, the welcoming of a new member of a community, saying goodbye to someone who is leaving, grieving a loss, or celebrating the beginning or end of a project or career. Is there an important turning of cycle that you, your friends, family, or community are experiencing? Perhaps all or part of your Solstice celebration could be used to honor it.

The ceremony is, as Lynda Paladin says in her book *Ceremonies for Change*, "your chance to speak to the subconscious mind in a symbolic manner, much as it does to you in your dreams."[7] Find appropriate symbols of what it is that you wish to activate or release. Often, common objects can serve to represent the key to the cycle of change you wish to celebrate: a feather or candle flame may represent spirit; a butterfly, transformation; a circle, completion or unity; a cup, nourishment or abundance; smoke, purification; a seed, potential for growth, hope, or an idea.

Once you have a symbol, decide upon a symbolic action to take with respect to it. The act of release may be symbolized in burning, tearing, burying, or giving away. Passage may be represented by moving the symbol from one place to another, by stepping over a boundary, bathing, or purifying with sage smoke. Affirmation can be expressed by placing the symbol on an altar or in a special container, or by unveiling it.

In addition to activities involving symbols, the ceremony may include other consciousness-focusing elements. You might wish to select an appropriate quotation, prayer, or blessing to read or recite at a fitting moment during the ritual. You may also wish to mark the boundaries of the ceremony in time and space, defining the borders of an area with a symbolic substance like cornmeal or water, or synchronizing the opening or closing of the ceremony with the movement of the Sun or Moon in relation to the horizon. Open the ceremony with a statement of intent, describing the purpose of the ceremony. Share a small amount of food and drink, affirming your common intent with a toast or by feeding one another a bit of food. Close the ceremony by centering your attention on the new reality toward which you seek to move. This moment is a symbolic rebirth and a renewal of your world, so mark and celebrate it accordingly with singing, hugs, and laughter.

A successful ceremony is in some respects also a good show. It is engaging and enjoyable as well as meaningful. Take care to include all the senses through movement (dance, gesture), sound (drumming, singing, rattles, bells) taste (herbs and foods that are bitter, sweet, sour, or salty), smell (flowers, essential oils, incense), touch (holding of hands, passing of ritual objects), and visual interest (through the design and decoration of the ritual space, colors, and fabric).

The most successful ceremonies are those that are woven into the day's other activities, and that are relevant to the concerns of all present. For example, I recall a recent summer Solstice celebration organized by a rural commune of about fifteen people who live on 350 acres in western Sonoma County. The community runs environmental education programs for children and hosts conferences for ecologists and herbalists. Each year for the past decade they've held a Solstice festival in June; this time, about sixty came. Shortly after noon, a community member blew a conch, signalling everyone to begin moving toward Solstice Hill, a circular mound with a spectacular view to the ocean. We formed a procession, passing through a gate where we were smudged with sage smoke. As we arrived at the hilltop, we formed a circle around a prepared altar. One of the community members, equipped with mask and rattle, enacted a Native American story about Coyote. Someone else led us in a song, and then began passing a pitcher of water around the circle. The water, always a precious resource in northern California, served to symbolize nature's nourishing power and also her vulnerability. Each member of the circle in turn ritually anointed her- or himself with a handful of water, then voiced a hope or prayer for the future. The prayers ranged from the personal to the universal; from simply "having a creative and happy summer" to longings for the protection of the Earth, the animals, and native peoples. After another song, the group joined in a spiral dance to the accompaniment of a strong drumbeat. In all, the ceremony lasted about two hours. The remainder of the afternoon was given to food (a pot luck lunch) and music.

Many ideas for specific ceremonies and rituals are included in *The Spiral Dance* by Starhawk and *Feeding the Spirit* by Nancy Brady Cunningham (see Bibliography).

The Give-away

One ceremony that is particularly suited to Solstice celebrations is the give-away, in which each participant brings and receives a gift.

The give-away described below is an adaptation of a widespread tribal custom. In agricultural villages in many parts of the world, any yearly food surplus is distributed at seasonal festivals. In some cases, the surplus goes first to a headman who, acting as trustee of the people, gives it away at a feast. He acquires status or prestige in this way, and so competing headmen may vie to see, not who can accumulate the most wealth, but who can give the most gifts.

For the Native American nations of the plains and the Pacific Northwest, give-aways were an ancient and essential feature of tribal economy. White settlers of the nineteenth century, however, saw these festivals as a threat to the capitalist values that their own government was then seeking to instill into the Native population. The give-away and the *potlatch* (the name for the practice among the nations of the Northwest) were discouraged and even legally banned, and Indians often resorted to heroic measures to continue the custom in the face of persecution and punishment.

In many tribal societies, no prestige flowed from wealth per se; indeed, to keep a surplus while anyone else was in need was considered shameful. In most societies that practiced the give-away, the socialist maxim of "from each according to ability, to each according to need" was put into practice far more effectively than was the case in any of the failed industrialized communist nations of the twentieth century. In the tribe, communal values were neither decreed nor enforced by a centralized authority, but had deep roots in culture and were spontaneously preserved and expressed in the course of daily life in every family and village.

The Solstice festival is an ideal occasion for the revival of the give-away. This may take the simplest of forms—as in bringing and exchanging gifts of food, clothing, and other useful items—or it may serve a more symbolic function, if each participant uses her gift to represent the essence of a current life change.

In the latter case, when the festival organizers send invitations to the event they should include instructions on how to choose a gift-symbol. The selected object should serve as the basis for a story—the story of that participant's recent or current challenge, victory, passage, or loss. The symbol is a marker of a life transition, a way of releasing stored energies and of affirming growth. If the experience being symbolized is a painful one, the object chosen should represent its real or desired resolution. After all, this object is about to be given to another person; the idea is not simply to pass one's troubles on to someone else, but to offer the recipient the opportunity to share in one's process of struggle and transformation.

As participants arrive at the event, the festival organizers indicate where to place their symbols—on a blanket in the center of the room or at the center of a bounded ritual space (if the event is being held outdoors). Then, when everyone has arrived, all sit in a circle around the gifts and the ceremony is convened with prayer, song, or reading. One of the organizers carefully selects an object, then asks who is giving it and what story it tells. The participant who brought it tells its story. Then the recipient of the gift tells why she chose it and what it means to her. The giver becomes the next receiver, selecting an object and asking for its story. And so it goes until each one present has given and received a gift.

In a large group it may be necessary to establish a time limit for stories. Often, the gift turns out to have as much symbolic relevance for the receiver as for the giver. The ceremony ends in a potluck feast with music and dance.

The Council of All Beings

You may wish to perform a ritual for a community that extends beyond the human species to the whole interlinked community of life on planet Earth by using the occasion of the Solstice to dramatize your group's collective grief and hope for nature and culture. A powerful ritual of this kind is the Council of All Beings, developed by Joanna Macy, John Seed, and Pat Fleming.

The Council is adaptable to a wide variety of settings; the numbers participating may range from fewer than a dozen to more than one hundred, and may include people of all ages (children under the age of ten will require childcare periodically during the process); its duration can be as short as an hour-and-a-half or as long as four days.

The essential purpose of the Council is to enable participants to express and channel the grief, despair, and anger that so many of us feel as we see the Earth and her creatures being destroyed before our eyes. Our usual tendency is to deny our feelings and lapse into numbness because we fear that nothing we can do will really help, or that our feelings, if acknowledged, would overwhelm us. John Seed writes that

This refusal of feeling takes a heavy toll on us, impoverishing both our emotional and our sensory lives. . . . Experience with group work has shown that this despair, grief and anger can be confronted, experienced and creatively channelled. Far from being crushed by it, new energy, creativity and empowerment can be released. Unblocking these feelings also opens us to experiencing our fundamental interconnectedness with all life. Often after such experiences, people come together to form ongoing support groups or join existing groups to take action on peace and/or environmental issues.[8]

The Council has three basic elements: mourning, remembering, and speaking from the perspective of other life-forms.

Mourning may take the form of telling eco-stories—each participant recounting a life experience in which she felt deeply connected with the natural world and/or experienced pain over what is befalling it. Or, participants may take turns reading from a list of endangered species; following each name, one of the group strikes together a pair of sticks or clackers, providing an auditory reminder of the finality of extinction. After the reading, leaders encourage participants to express their feelings of honor for these passing species, or of grief at their loss. Other exercises for the evocation of mourning can be adapted from ones described by Joanna Macy in her *Despair and Personal Power in the Nuclear Age*.

Exercises of *remembering* are intended to help us recall our planet's own story and the untold millennia of human prehistory and history during which we humans lived in sacred interdependence with other living things. Participants may share in the reading of creation myths from the world's cultures (as a source, use Barbara Sproul's *Primal Myths*). Then, a leader invites the participants into a guided movement meditation: a narrator recites the basic stages of the evolutionary development of life on Earth—from the cellular to the reptilian to the mammalian—and at each stage participants are encouraged to imagine themselves as existing at that stage of life and to move accordingly. Some may choose to sit quietly. At the end of the exercise (which should take about an hour) allow time for people in pairs to describe to each other how it felt to remember being trilobite or lizard or small mammal. As an alternative to these exercises, read aloud "Our Life as Gaia" by Joanna Macy in *Thinking Like a Mountain*.

The Council climaxes in the process of *identifying with another life-form*. After spending time alone, taking on the identities of natural beings, the participants make masks; then they smudge themselves in sage smoke, anoint themselves with fresh water, and begin the ritual. Turning to each of the four directions, they invoke the powers of nature and the beings of the Three Times—those who have nurtured the Earth in the past, those who are saving it in the present, and those of the future for whom the Earth is being preserved. Each being in turn speaks for itself and its kind: "I am ant; I am bear; I am mountain; I am lichen." A few of the participants remove their masks and sit in the circle's center to represent humankind and listen to the stories of the others.

> I am rainforest. . . . You destroy me so carelessly, tearing down so many of my trees for a few planks. . . . You cause my thick layer of precious topsoil to wash away, destroying the coral reefs that fringe me. . . . Your screaming machines tear through my trunks, rip my flesh, reducing me to sawdust and furniture.[9]

At last a human speaks. "We hear you, fellow beings. We feel overwhelmed. We need your help. Are there powers you can share with us in this hard time?" Each being offers its unique strength as a source of help for the others, then removes its mask and joins the humans in the center. The humans hum as one organism, then conclude the Council. The closing cannot be planned in detail, since its nature will depend on the dynamics of what has gone before. The life forms invoked should be ritually released with thanks; afterward, either meditation and sharing of individual experiences or singing and dancing may be in order.

As preparation for leading a Council of All Beings, read Chapter 4 of Joanna Macy's *Despair and Personal Power in the Nuclear Age*, and "Guidelines for a Council of All Beings Workshop" by Joanna Macy and Pat Fleming in *Thinking Like a Mountain*.

The June Solstice—A Festival of the Divine Feminine

In Chapter 9 we called the June Solstice (the summer Solstice in the northern hemisphere) the forgotten festival. We also noted the need in our modern Western culture for a festival of the divine feminine. I would like to propose, therefore, to regard the June Solstice as a festival of the feminine spirit and of nature—of the animals, herbs, flowers, trees, grasses, and birds.

As we have seen, the December Solstice carries with it the mythic residue of many centuries of Christmas and New Year observances. These associations are helpful in that they provide points of connection back to the Neolithic Solstice rites of our ancestors. But they also serve somewhat to inhibit the free creativity of our celebration in the present: there will always be the need to define for oneself or one's friends or family the distinctions and similarities between Solstice festivals and Christmas and New Year rites. For European-Americans, the June Solstice has few remaining cultural associations. It is virtually a blank slate inviting our playful ingenuity. It therefore offers a unique opportunity for cultural renewal in which anyone may participate.

The June Solstice can be a day on which to honor the Goddess in all her names, forms, and guises—Mary, Gaia, Isis, Inanna, Hathor, Ceres, Ishtar, Sophia, Kali, Kuan-Yin, Amaterasu, Oshun, Buffalo Calf Woman, Demeter, Spider Woman, Parvati, Lakshmi, Magna Mater, etc. As preparation for the June festival, read about ancient goddess religions in Carl Olson's anthology *The Book of the Goddess Past and Present*, or in Merlin Stone's classic *When God Was a Woman*.

The June Solstice might also be an occasion to celebrate the *yin* qualities of being—nourishing, uniting, spontaneous, not judging. While *yang* pertains to individualization, *yin* focuses on relationship; where *yang* is causal and sequential, *yin* is acausal and simultaneous. *Yin* is related to eros, which Carl Jung regarded as the archetype of relatedness. Eros nourishes and embraces all beings, offering uncritical protection and support. But it is also passionate, wild, sensuous, irrational, and ecstatic. In her negative aspect, the goddess is she who dissolves form back into chaos.

The June Solstice may also serve as a time to remember women in history. Of course, most of history as presently told is about struggles for control of land and resources; it is the past as viewed by the powerful and victorious. Little wonder, then, that our history books are filled with the names of men, women usually being mentioned only in supportive roles. But history often takes on more meaning and interest when we deliberately assume the viewpoint of conquered or subordinated peoples—such as the Native Americans, African Americans, or women. As Riane Eisler notes in *The Chalice and the Blade*, history has known cycles in which harsh, repressive, "androcratic" values alternated with creative, egalitarian, "gylanic" ones. She cites the early Christian period, the troubadour period in southern France, the Elizabethan period in England, the Italian Renaissance, and the French Enlightenment as examples of historical moments when women were granted greater freedom, access to education, and social influence, or when "feminine" values were in the ascendancy, as evidenced by reduced social and sexual repression and an increased emphasis on the arts.

Women who have shaped history and culture range from Themestoclea and Diotema (the teachers of Pythagoras and Socrates), to the poet Sappho, to the medieval herbalist Hildegard of Bingen, to the mystic Julian of Norwich, to the humanitarian Florence Nightingale, to nineteenth-century feminists like Lucy Stone, Margaret Fuller, Mary Lyon, Elizabeth Cady Stanton, and Susan B. Anthony, to writers like George Sand, Maya Angelou, Rachel Carson, Simone de Beauvoir, Emily Dickinson, Alice Walker, Helen Keller, and Gertrude Stein. At your June Solstice festival, you may wish to read aloud from women's writings, or to read a brief biography of a woman you admire.

In order to be an authentic celebration of the divine feminine, a June Solstice festival should have women in primary roles as celebrants and planners. Men needn't be excluded, but avoid leaving the decisionmaking in their hands.

As we noted in Chapter 8, fire has often played a significant role in June Solstice festivals. Perhaps that is because fire so well symbolizes both transformation and the dissolution of form into chaos—positive and negative aspects of the divine feminine. Find a way to include fire in your ceremony or festival, if only by way of a candle. But be careful: if you wish to build a campfire or bonfire, make sure you are violating no local ordinances and that you take all reasonable safety precautions.

Any of the activities we have suggested thus far in Chapters 10 and 11 may be used in a June Solstice festival—singing and dancing, cooperative games, a Council of All Beings, a give-away, a life-passage ceremony, etc. The divine feminine principle comes to the fore primarily by way of nuance and intent. Midwinter is naturally more a time for introspection—for examining your life direction and renewing your commitments; while Midsummer is more a time for emotional release. For your June festival, make an extra effort to find ways to include the eros archetype via song, dance, food, and play. Spend as much of your day as possible outdoors, and make the Earth, the trees, the animals, and the herbs co-celebrants.

We live at a delicate and dangerous time in history. At the dawn of the third millennium, we find ourselves threatened not so much by wars or sudden and overwhelming natural catastrophes (though these, as always, are possible) as by an accelerating erosion of culture. We know how somewhat to heal the wounds of battle, fire, earthquake, and hurricane. But we are mute and helpless before the gradually accumulating crises being brought on by our own lifestyles and values.

The greatest single crisis that faces us is overpopulation—not just in the Third World, where sheer rates of increase are higher, but also in the affluent countries, where each incremental net gain in population constitutes a disproportionate drain on the world's resources. One of the primary characteristics of a healthy and successful culture is that it keeps the size of its human population stable. But repeatedly in the last ten thousand years cultures have exceeded the limits of their environment's ability to sustain life, always with dire consequences.

Ever since the invention of farming, population pressure has served as a decisive factor in the rise and fall of civilizations. Now, having created the first truly global economy, we are in the process of joining every patch of arable land on the planet into one great feedlot for our vast and burgeoning human population. We have created a civilization from which there is no escape. The consequent loss of wilderness and of human cultural depth and diversity is incalculable.

We need help in dealing with all of this furious and often unsettling change. We need cultural forms to help us celebrate life in the midst of suffering and death. Now, perhaps more than ever, we need festivals to bring us together, to help us heal ourselves and our world, to help us restore nature and culture.

Celebrating the Solstices could play an important role in our efforts toward cultural renewal. But a seasonal festival is no end in itself. Perhaps one day, if we are able to rediscover the wellsprings of culture, we will regain the fully timeless and spontaneous openness to life that our Paleolithic gatherer-hunter forebears knew. For them, the seasons required no measurement or record keeping, and they were experienced more in the behavior of animals, in the smell, taste, and appearance of plants, and in rain, heat, and the quality of the wind, than in the motions of the Sun.

But we are far from that condition now. We are doubly alienated: if the adoption of agriculture drove the initial wedge between humankind and nature, industrialism has widened the gap to a yawning gulf. From where we stand, we cannot all return to nature in a single heroic leap; we must first reforge our ancient ties to soil and place, to trees and birds, to seasons and cycles, and to nourishing human communities. Perhaps celebrating the Solstices will trigger instinctual memories of the Neolithic, when the Great Goddess presided over an age more peaceful and creative than our own. And then, having learned from that recollection, so that our hands, eyes, ears, and hearts once more respond to natural materials and rhythms, we may find ourselves awakening to memories that lie deeper still. But that is likely to be a process whose ultimate fulfillment lies many generations to come. It is our role not so much to reap the benefits of cultural regeneration as to scatter its seeds, and to find our reward in the sowing.

So now let us rejoice, for we are alive, and life is good. However you choose to celebrate—alone or with friends or family, in the wilderness or in the city, in summer or in winter—may all your Solstices be times of renewal.

NOTES

Chapter Three

1. See Gay Gaer Luce, *Biological Rhythms in Human & Animal Physiology*, p. 13.
2. Ibid., pp. 44 ff.
3. Ibid., p. 128.
4. Ibid., p. 66.
5. Ibid., p. 123.
6. Jeremy Rifkin, *Time Wars*, p. 3.
7. E. C. Krupp, *Echoes of the Ancient Skies*, p. 164.
8. Jean Hunt, *Tracking the Flood Survivors*.
9. Quoted in Evan Hadingham, *Early Man and the Cosmos*, p. 51.
10. Quoted in Anne Bancroft, *The Origins of the Sacred*, pp. 50–51.
11. E. C. Krupp, ed., *In Search of Ancient Astronomies*.

Chapter Four

1. Norman Lockyer, *The Dawn of Astronomy*, p. 99.
2. Ibid., p. 198.
3. Ibid., p. 85. Lockyer's conclusions were later questioned by archaeoastronomer Gerald Hawkins, who cited observations by a British Army engineer in 1891 that showed that the western Theban hills block the summer Solstice sunset rays from entering the Temple. Hawkins suggested that the structure was oriented instead toward winter Solstice sunrise, and indicated similar alignments elsewhere in the Temple complex.
4. E. A. Wallis Budge, *The Gods of the Egyptians*, Vol. II, p. 47.
5. Ibid., in his Preface to Lockyer, p. ix.
6. Mircea Eliade, *Cosmos and History*, p. 52.
7. Norman Lockyer, *opus cit.*, p. 93.

Chapter Five

1. See Evan Hadingham, *Early Man and the Cosmos*, p. 88.

2. Thomas E. Mails, *Secret Native American Pathways: A Guide to Inner Peace*, p. 190. See also Joseph Epes Brown and Black Elk, *The Sacred Pipe*.
3. Quoted in James Cornell, *The First Stargazers*, p. 159.
4. Quoted in ibid., p. 160.
5. Quoted in Hadingham, *op. cit.*, p. 131.
6. Quoted in Beck and Walters, *The Sacred*, p. 94.
7. Ralph L. Roys, *The Book of Chilam Balam of Chumael*, p. 86.
8. Ptolemy Tompkins, *This Tree Grows out of Hell*, pp. 60–61.
9. Quoted in Hadingham, *op. cit.*, p. 170.
10. E. C. Krupp, *Echoes of Ancient Skies*, pp. 199–200.
11. E. C. Krupp, *op. cit.*, p. 241.

Chapter Six

1. Norman Lockyer, *The Dawn of Astronomy*, p. 88.
2. In his Introduction to the Surya Siddhanta, transl. Ebenezer Burgess. Calcutta, 1935, p. viii. Quoted in Rupert Gleadow, *The Zodiac*, p. 142.
3. Martha Beckwith, *Hawaiian Mythology*, p. 119.

Chapter Seven

1. Hilda Kuper, *The Swazi: A South African Kingdom*, p. 70.
2. Theodor H. Gaster, Introduction to James G. Frazer, *The New Golden Bough*, pp. xix–xx.
3. Editorial note in James G. Frazer, *The Illustrated Golden Bough*, Mary Douglas, general ed., 1978, p. 18.
4. Ibid., p. 10.
5. James G. Frazer, from the Synopsis to *The New Golden Bough*, pp. xxi–xxiv.
6. James G. Frazer, *The Illustrated Golden Bough*, Mary Douglas, general ed., p. 234.
7. S. H. Hooke, *Middle Eastern Mythology*, p. 39.
8. Theodore H. Gaster, *New Year: Its History, Customs and Superstition*, p. xi.

9. Helmut Gipper, in R. Pinxten, ed., *Universalism and Relativism in Language and Thought*, p. 226.
10. James G. Frazer, *The Illustrated Golden Bough*, p. 189.

Chapter Eight

1. See Margaret Murray, *The Witch-Cult in Western Europe.*
2. William Marlin, "When Ancient Basilica Becomes a Sundial."
3. E. C. Krupp, *Beyond the Blue Horizon*, pp. 302–303.
4. Pius Parsch, *The Church's Year of Grace*, v. 4, p. 204.
5. James G. Frazer, *The Illustrated Golden Bough*, p. 229.
6. James G. Frazer, *The New Golden Bough*, p. 230.
7. Dolores LaChapelle, *Earth Wisdom*, p. 169.
8. Quoted in James G. Frazer, *The New Golden Bough*, p. 710.
9. Ibid., p. 737.
10. Jacqueline Simpson, *European Mythology*, p. 136.
11. James G. Frazer, *The New Golden Bough*, p. 716.
12. Ibid., p. 125.
13. Dolores LaChapelle, *Sacred Land, Sacred Sex*; Georg Feuerstein, *Sacred Sexuality.*
14. LaChapelle, *op. cit.*, p. 263.
15. James G. Frazer, *The New Golden Bough*, p. 231.
16. Ibid.

Chapter Nine

1. *I Ching*, Wilhelm/Baynes, pp. 97–98.
2. *The Paleolithic Prescription*, p. 211.
3. See Annette Hamilton, *Nature and Nurture: Aboriginal Child-rearing in North-central Arnhem Land.*
4. *The Paleolithic Prescription*, p. 207.
5. Dolores LaChapelle, *Sacred Land, Sacred Sex: Rapture of the Deep*, p. 254.
6. Mircea Eliade, *Rites and Symbols of Initiation: The Mysteries of Birth and Rebirth*, p. 25.
7. LaChapelle, p. 253.
8. Robert Lawlor, *Voices of the First Day*, p. 229.

9. Lewis Hodous, *Folkways in China.*

10. LaChapelle, *op. cit.*, p. 267.

Chapter Ten

1. John Michell, *The New View over Atlantis*, p. 84.

Chapter Eleven

1. Alfie Kohn, *No Contest*, p. 91.

2. Terry Orlick, *The Cooperative Sports and Games Book*, p. 31.

3. Jeffrey Sobel, *Everybody Wins*, p. 53.

4. Terry Orlick, *The Second Cooperative Sports and Games Book*, p. 231.

5. Allan and Paulette Macfarlan, *Handbook of American Indian Games*, p. 253.

6. Available from Serpentine Music, P.O. Box 1667, Forestville, CA 95436.

7. Lynda Palladin, *Ceremonies for Change*, p. 56. Many of the suggestions in this section are drawn from this useful book, which focuses specifically on the personal use of ritual and ceremony to mark significant life changes.

8. John Seed, Joanna Macy, Pat Fleming, Arne Naess, *Thinking Like a Mountain: Towards a Council of All Beings*, p. 8.

9. Ibid., pp. 85–8.

BIBLIOGRAPHY

Anderson, William. *The Green Man: The Archetype of our Oneness with the Earth.* London: HarperCollins, 1990.

Andruss, Van, et al., eds. *Home! A Bioregional Reader.* Santa Cruz: New Society, 1990.

Aveni, Anthony. *Empires of Time: Calendars, Clocks, and Cultures.* New York: Basic Books, 1989.

Bancroft, Anne. *Origins of the Sacred: The Spiritual Journey in Western Tradition.* London: Arkana, 1987.

Beard, Mary. *Woman as a Force in History.* New York: Macmillan, 1946.

Beck, Peggy V., and Anna L. Walters. *The Sacred: Ways of Knowledge, Sources of Life.* Navajo Nation: Navajo Community College, 1977.

Becker, Robert O., and Gary Selden. *The Body Electric: Electromagnetism and the Foundation of Life.* New York: Morrow, 1985.

Beckwith, Martha. *Hawaiian Mythology.* Honolulu: University of Hawaii Press, 1970.

Berg, Peter. *Figures of Regulation: Guides for Re-Balancing Society with the Biosphere.* San Francisco: Planet Drum Foundation, n.d.

Black Elk, with Joseph Epes Brown. *The Sacred Pipe: Black Elk's Account of the Seven Rites of the Oglala Sioux.* New York: Penguin, 1971.

Brown, Peter Lancaster. *Megaliths, Myths and Men: An Introduction to Astro-Archaeology.* New York: Taplinger, 1976.

Brown, Tom, with Brandt Morgan. *Tom Brown's Field Guide to Nature Observation and Tracking.* New York: Berkley, 1983.

Budge, E. A. Wallis. *The Gods of the Egyptians.* New York: Dover, 1969 (reprint).

Calvin, William H. *How the Shaman Stole the Moon: In Search of Ancient Prophet-Scientists from Stonehenge to the Grand Canyon.* New York: Bantam, 1991.

Campbell, R. J. *The Story of Christmas.* New York: Macmillan, 1934.

Cooke, Ian. *Mermaid to Merrymaid, Journey to the Stones: Nine Walks to Ancient Sites in the Land's End Peninsula, Cornwall.* Penzance: Men-an-Tol Studio, 1987.

Cornell, James. *The First Stargazers: An Introduction to the Origins of Astronomy.* New York: Scribner's, 1981.

Cunningham, Nancy Brady. *Feeding the Spirit.* San Jose: Resource Publications, 1988.

Devereux, Paul. *Places of Power.* London: Blandford, 1990.

Donaldson, O. Fred. *Playing by Heart: The Vision and Practice of Belonging.* Deerfield Beach, Florida: Health Communications, 1993.

Eisler, Riane. *The Chalice and the Blade: Our History, Our Future.* San Francisco: Harper & Row, 1987.

Ereira, Alan. *Elder Brothers.* New York: Knopf, 1992.

Eliade, Mircea. *Cosmos and History: The Myth of the Eternal Return.* New York: Harper & Row, 1959.

————. *Rites and Symbols of Initiation: The Mysteries of Birth and Rebirth.* New York: Harper & Row, 1958.

Feuerstein, Georg. *Sacred Sexuality: Living the Vision of the Erotic Spirit.* Los Angeles: Tarcher, 1992.

Foley, Daniel J. *The Christmas Tree.* Philadelphia: Chilton, 1960.

Frazer, Sir James George. Mary Douglas, ed. *The Illustrated Golden Bough.* Garden City, N.Y.: Doubleday, 1978.

————. Theodor H. Gaster, ed. *The New Golden Bough.* New York: Mentor, 1964.

Gaster, Theodor H. *New Year: Its History, Customs, and Superstitions.* New York: Abelard-Schuman, 1955.

Gipper, Helmut, in R. Pinxten, ed. *Universalism and Relativism in Language and Thought.* The Hague: Mouton, 1976, p. 226.

Gleadow, Rupert. *The Origin of the Zodiac.* New York: Athenium, 1969.

Hadingham, Evan. *Early Man and the Cosmos.* New York: Walker, 1984.

Hamilton, Annette. *Nature and Nurture: Aboriginal Child-rearing in North-central Arnhem Land.* Canberra: Australian Institute for Aboriginal Studies, 1981.

Hart, Mickey. *Drumming at the Edge of Magic: A Journey into the Spirit of Percussion.* San Francisco: Harper, 1990.

Heinberg, Richard. *Memories and Visions of Paradise: Exploring the Universal Myth of a Lost Golden Age.* Los Angeles: Tarcher, 1989.

Hudson, Travis, and Ernest Underhay. *Crystals in the Sky: An Intellectual Odyssey Involving Chumash Astronomy, Cosmology and Rock Art.* Socorro, New Mexico: Ballena Press, 1978.

Hunt, Jean. *Tracking the Flood Survivors.* Shreveport, Louisiana: Hunt, 1988.

Imber-Black, Evan, and Janine Roberts. *Rituals for Our Times: Celebrating, Healing, and Changing Our Lives and Our Relationships.* New York: HarperCollins, 1992.

Karas, Sheryl Ann. *The Solstice Evergreen.* Lower Lake, Calif.: Aslan, 1991.

Kohn, Alfie. *No Contest: The Case Against Competition.* Boston: Houghton Mifflin, 1992 (second edition).

Krupp, E. C., ed. *In Search of Ancient Astronomies.* Garden City: Doubleday, 1977.

———. *Beyond the Blue Horizon.* New York: HarperCollins, 1991.

———. *Echoes of Ancient Skies.* New York: Harper & Row, 1983.

Kuper, Hilda. *An African Aristocracy.* London: Oxford University Press, 1969.

———. *The Swazi: A South African Kingdom.* New York: Holt, Rinehart and Winston, 1964.

LaChapelle, Dolores. *Earth Wisdom.* Silverton, Colo.: Finn Hill Arts, 1978.

———. *Sacred Land, Sacred Sex: Rapture of the Deep.* Durango: Kikaví, 1988; 2nd printing 1992.

———. *Earth Festivals.* Silverton, Colo. : Finn Hill Arts, 1976.

Lockyer, J. Norman. *The Dawn of Astronomy.* Cambridge: M.I.T. Press, 1964. (First edition, London: Cassell, 1894).

Luce, Gay Gaer. *Biological Rhythms in Human & Animal Physiology.* New York: Dover, 1971.

Macy, Joanna. *Despair and Personal Power in the Nuclear Age.* Santa Cruz: New Society Publishers, 1983.

Mails, Thomas E. *Secret Native American Pathways: A Guide to Inner Peace.* Tulsa, Oklahoma: Council Oak Books, 1988.

Margolin, Malcolm. *The Earth Manual: How to Work on Wild Land Without Taming It.* Berkeley: Heyday, 1985.

Marlin, William. "When Ancient Basilica Becomes a Sundial." *The Christian Science Monitor,* January 21, 1977.

Merchant, Carolyn. *Radical Ecology: The Search for a Livable World.* New York: Routledge, 1992.

Michell, John. *A Little History of Astro-Archaeology.* London: Thames & Hudson, 1989.

———. *The New View Over Atlantis.* San Francisco: Harper & Row, 1986.

Miles, Clement A. *Christmas Customs and Traditions: Their History and Significance.* New York: Dover, 1976.

Mills, Stephanie. *Whatever Happened to Ecology?* San Francisco: Sierra, 1989.

Murray, Margaret A. *The Witch-Cult in Western Europe.* New York: Oxford University Press, 1971.

Olson, Carl, ed. *The Book of the Goddess Past and Present.* New York: Crossroad, 1989.

O'Neil, W. M. *Time and the Calendars.* Sydney: Sydney University Press, 1975.

Paladin, Lynda S. *Ceremonies for Change: Creating Personal Ritual to Heal Life's Hurts.* Walpole, NH: Stillpoint, 1991.

Pike, Royston. *Round the Year with the World's Religions.* New York: Schuman, 1950.

Rifkin, Jeremy. *Time Wars: The Primary Conflict in Human History.* New York: Henry Holt, 1987.

Roys, Ralph L. *The Book of Chilam Balam of Chumael.* Norman, Oklahoma: University of Oklahoma Press, 1967.

Seed, John; Joanna Macy, Pat Fleming, and Arne Naess. *Thinking Like a Mountain: Towards a Council of All Beings.* Philadelphia: New Society Publishers, 1988.

Sobel, Jeffrey. *Everybody Wins: 393 Non-Competitive Games for Young Children.* New York: Walker, 1983.

Sproul, Barbara. *Primal Myths: Creating the World.* San Francisco: Harper & Row, 1979.

Starhawk. *The Spiral Dance: A Rebirth of the Ancient Religion of the Great Goddess.* San Francisco: Harper & Row, 1979.

———. *Truth or Dare: Encounters with Power, Authority, and Mystery.* San Francisco: Harper, 1987.

———. *Dreaming the Dark: Magic, Sex & Politics,* second ed. Boston: Beacon, 1988.

Stencel, Robert; F. Richard, and David H. Clark. "Astronomy and Cosmology in Angkor Wat." *Science,* 193(4520) [23 July, 1976], pp. 281-287.

Stone, Merlin. *When God Was a Woman.* New York: Harcourt Brace Jovanovich, 1976.

Swan, James A., ed. *The Power Of Place.* Wheaton, Il.: Quest, 1991.

Thurley, Elizabeth Fusae. *Through the Year in Japan.* London: Batsford, 1985.

Tompkins, Peter. *Mysteries of the Mexican Pyramids.* New York: Harper & Row, 1976.

———. *Secrets of the Great Pyramid.* New York: Harper & Row, 1971.

Tompkins, Ptolemy. *This Tree Grows out of Hell: Mesoamerica and the Search for the Magical Body.* San Francisco: Harper San Francisco, 1990.

Tree People, with Andy and Kate Lipkis. *The Simple Act of Planting a Tree.* Los Angeles: Tarcher, 1990.

Wilhelm, Richard, and Cary F. Baynes, trans. *The I Ching or Book of Changes.* Princeton: Princeton University Press (third edition), 1967.

INDEX